D0853130

Fight the
Wild Island

BY THE SAME AUTHOR

Beyond the Last Oasis

A Solo Walk in the Western Sahara

FIGHT THE WILD ISLAND

A Solo Walk across Iceland

Ted Edwards

SALEM HOUSE PUBLISHERS

TOPSFIELD, MASSACHUSETTS

© Ted Edwards 1986

First published in the United States
by Salem House Publishers, 1987, 462 Boston Street, Topsfield, MA 01983.

Printed in Great Britain

Library of Congress Catalog Card Number: 86–61744

ISBN: 0 88162 258 3

To the free people of Iceland,
who showed the world
that only the brave deserve to be free,
I dedicate this book.
Long may they enjoy
what they have wrought.

T.E., 1986

Contents

Illustrations

Acknowledgements

I wish to thank Judy Meakin for improving my English spelling; Lynda Simpson for her very fine maps; the Icelandic Tourist Board for their permission to reproduce photographs of Lake Öskjuvatn, Gullfoss, Strokkur and the City of Reykjavik; Phil Cusack for his permission to reproduce the photograph of me on the back flap of the jacket; Dick Phillips for various items of information; Survival Aids and Karrimor for equipment, and BBC North West for the loan of their cine-camera.

I would also like to extend my gratitude to the hardy and gentle people of Iceland for the welcome and hospitality they showed to their Lancastrian cousin.

Author's Note

The northern myths here set down are gathered from various branches of the tradition and cobbled together into a coherent whole to give a flavour of what the ancients believed and are in no way meant to be a gospel. Scholars may find them over-simplified and I accept this criticism. If this small taste brings forth appetite then get thee to a library.

Most personal and place names I have written in the Roman script to cut down on confusion; however I have retained the consonant *eth*, written ð or Ð as its distinctive pronunciation cannot be truly represented by an English *d*, *t* or *th* as pronounced south of the Manchester Ship Canal. Its pronunciation is the hard and sharp *th* of northern England as in *that*.

There are slight variations in the following vowels:

á is pronounced *ow* as in *cow*.
ó is pronounced *oh* as in *Oh*.
ö is pronounced *eu* as in the French *fleur*.
ú is pronounced *oo* as in *moon*.
ei is pronounced *ay* as in *play*.
But don't worry about 'em.

Ðat's ðat!

ROUTE OF TED EDWARDS
TRANS-ICELANDIC EXPEDITION
1984

The first crossing on foot;
510 miles in twenty-four days,
10 August–2 September 1984

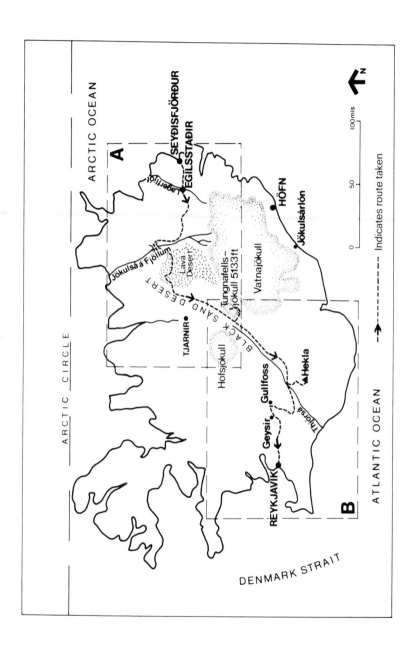

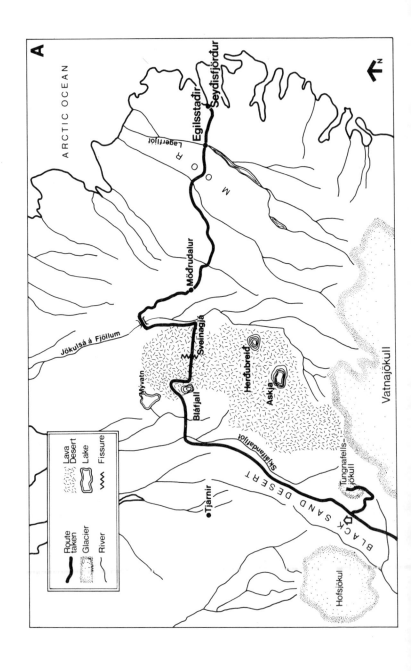

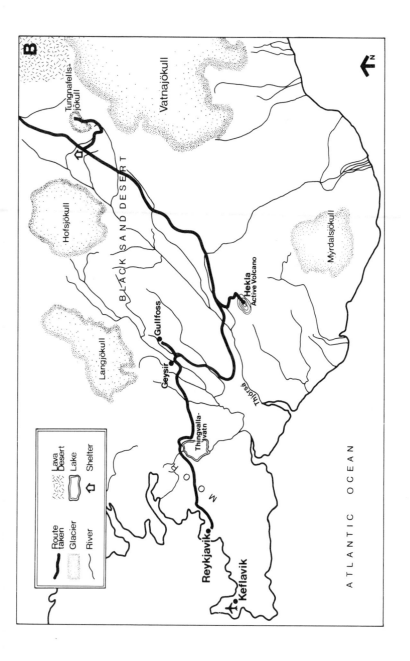

1 Heritage

Once there was a time, a thousand years and more ago, in a place we now call Lancashire, when a man whose name, perhaps, was Olaf, sat by his evening fire and was troubled in his mind. He would have been a young man whose veins ran with the blood of his father, dead in the service of Guthrum who had taken the land from the English. It was warrior blood, Viking blood, which had stained the soil of Russia, of Constantinople and of the Frankish heartlands to the south; and now it flowed through hands that sat uneasily upon the plough.

His hair was yellow and long, and braided in the way of the warrior, and at his side hung a warrior's sword; but it was clean and unstained, and his fair skin bore no marks of battle. About him were other fires from which came the sounds of settlement, the laughter of children and of women. Some were English women who harboured the alien christ-god in their breasts and taught his ways to the sons of Oðin. Even the mighty Guthrum paid homage to this foreign god and spoke to fighting men of husbandry and the tilling of the land.

The man whose name, perhaps, was Olaf, had taken to himself no wife for in his being was the restlessness of youth, the drive which had taken his father's young armies of conquest from the fjords to far lands. He had heard talk of a land towards the setting sun, beyond the island kingdom of Mann; and tales he had heard of other lands, new lands where kings held no sway. There was a place, so it was said, towards the northern star, where a man could be his own king and rule his own lands. In that place were mountains of fire and boiling lakes. Rivers of ice spread over great desert lands and strange and powerful creatures of the sea guarded its shores. *There was a land for warriors*, and in such a land even a plough was a kind of sword. Many, so the tellers of tales had said, were going there; and the name of the land was Iceland.

It may be that he thought of this land for a winter; it would not have been two, for a warrior owns an impetuous heart. Then there came a time for the gathering together of things to carry and, without looking back, this man whose name, perhaps, was Olaf, walked with a bounce in his step and the fire of living in his ice-blue eyes, towards the western coast of the foreign land which gave him birth.

Blackrod? My god! Where's Blackrod?

The train rushed north through the man-made Lancashire landscape, past black slag-heaps lately cosmetically greened, over holiday canals, by mills satanic and irredeemably dark, *gettin' away – gettin' away – gettin' away*. The little station of Blackrod vanished behind, a mark somewhere on the way to Preston, which was somewhere on the way to Glasgow, which was somewhere on the way to ...

My people were in Manchester, the people that I knew and could touch with confidence. I was alone. No – not utterly alone, for around me were my kind. Were I to ask, I would receive, but not to touch. That was the thing; to touch, casually and informally, on shoulder, on elbow, on hand. The lone challenge was what I sought; but – oh – the touch; already I missed despairingly the touch. It would go; in hours, in days, it would go. There would come a time very soon when it would go, and I would be a rock against the elements. But now I was not a rock. Now I missed the touch; and did not know if I would touch again.

PRESTON read the station sign as the station platform slid to a halt. I heaved my impossibly heavy rucksack onto my right shoulder and carefully eased it through doors and people, catching ice-axe on lintel and buckle on jacket. Seventy-two pounds, the scales had registered; seventy-two pounds of freeze-dried food, movie camera, survival equipment, tape-recorder, cooking gear, film, tape, battery, clothing, medical supplies, the list was endless, each item having had to prove, before the fiercest of judges, its inalienable right to be there. I had thrown out fully four and a half pounds of cardboard, paper and plastic packaging to lighten the load, but here, finally edited, was the concrete-solid seventy-two pounds with which I must begin my four-hundred-mile-plus trek across Iceland, from the east coast to the sea of the western shore.

And why was I undertaking this journey which I knew even then would be the most physically demanding of all my journeys to date? It would not be of substantial benefit to mankind, nor push back the frontiers of knowledge as had previous excursions. No great financial reward would be mine, nor crown of glory rest upon my head. No, this journey would be undertaken for the best and ultimately most sensible of reasons; because it was my wish to undertake it. But *wishing* alone is for children, so *excuses* must be carried, and these must be called *reasons*. That I had never set foot on a glacier, seen an active volcano or geyser, traversed a lava desert, these were great incentives to one endowed with curiosity. There was also money to be made on a mile-by-mile sponsorship basis for a local children's hospital, promised upon forms in pubs, clubs and work-places by the good people of Manchester upon the completion of my journey.

But my main reason, the one that has spanned all my expeditions, was to show that such a journey was possible for one man using light-weight modern equipment. A very few years ago it would have been made impossible by the sheer weight and bulk of that which must be carried. Now, thanks to research and development, we are entering a new era of exploration which does not require large expensive expeditions but can be conducted by a lone explorer with his own personal mission. It is the pioneering of this attitude that my journeys in inaccessible parts of the world have been principally about.

The Glasgow train absorbed the waiting hotchpotch of humanity, each on his own private journey, and wrote a swift line north over Shap, cool and dank with dark clouds about it, showing no respect for early August. Tattered Scottish pounds, lettuce-limp and foreign, were placed with sandwiches in my hand by the brogue-spoken buffet car assistant. Already the world was changing about me as I was *gettin' away – gettin' away – gettin' away.*

Glasgow seemed to be a remarkably unremarkable city as I picked my tottering way out of the railway station to the airport bus. Just another western city of bricks and concrete, pretentious pseudo-Greek pillars and insular bustle. My mind was split between Manchester and Iceland as my body boarded the coach and left it, and went through the familiar formalities of foreign flight. What would my people be doing now? Was the hole left by my non-presence already filling? Was it important, now that for one month I would not be living that life, but another life on another plane of existence with different purposes and routines and values? To live the life of a vagabond, each night to rest in another space, requires a different bargain with life. Insecurity must be relished, but reliance placed upon that greater security – the confidence in one's own ability to survive.

'Will passengers for flight four-four-three-three to Reykjavik please board at gate number four. Passengers for Reykjavik board at gate number four. Thank you.'

The efficient female voice caused bustle and fuss in the departure lounge as bags were gathered, children retrieved and parties assembled. Young hardy men in tartan shirts and scarred climbing boots, elderly couples full of tentative wonderment, neat businessmen with slim executive cases, camera-bedecked tourists in stiff new clothes, all moved slowly in file down the long corridor following the signs for gate number four, speaking in English, Icelandic and American.

The aircraft, sleek and shining on the darkened concrete, accepted us all up its stairway and we sat, waiting, strapped, watching the stewardesses perform the ballet of the life-jacket. Hydraulics hissed and engines whistled as the plane trundled along the taxiway. A great roar of sheer power shook our mini-world as we sprang down the runway, faster and faster, concrete battering tyres; then the nose raised itself a little and the world was calm and smooth again. We had left Britain. The toy-town lights of Glasgow dropped away and were gone. Ahead was the North Atlantic and Iceland. Ahead was adventure and battle; but the touch – ah yes – the touch; how I missed the touch.

Iceland is a volcanic island slightly bigger than Ireland sitting just south of the arctic circle in the North Atlantic. Over 200 million years ago the surface of the young planet was cooling. The natural laws decreed that the cooling surface become solid. The higher portion became a mighty single land-mass and the lower sank beneath condensing vapour to become sea bed. But below the cooling surface the planet was yet molten and seething with the heat of Hell. The thin surface cracked and the land split into several continents. One drifted to the west, forced ponderously away from its neighbours as the molten core belched to the surface. The waters entered the mighty gap and the constantly flowing lava, cooled by their wetness, formed a great ridge between the continents, ever pushing upwards towards the surface. The dinosaurs came and went and bird-song was heard on the land. And still the ridge grew in the depths of the ocean. Time after time ice covered the planet, and ape-creatures began to appear. Finally, about the time of the last age of ice, some sixteen million years before men called the ocean Atlantic, the ridge broke the surface and amid fire, smoke and steam, a new island of the north had its tempestuous birth.

There the land lay, alone and unpeopled, whilst the planet grew older. Ice formed upon its cooling slopes; and seeds carried by migrating birds, friendly winds and convenient ocean currents began to sprout, adding green to the grey and the white.

In the eighth century Irish monks, in search of solitude, came upon the unexpected land, and reared sheep there to sustain their meditations. Early in the ninth century, when the great Viking expansion west had begun to populate the north of England, the Isle of Man, the Faroes and Ireland, the Viking sailors found Iceland still dotted with a few sheep and monks. So from these settlements, and from mainland Scandinavia, went settlers to till its green coastal regions. The Vikings who stayed in the north of England gave us a linguistic heritage that became the Lancashire and Yorkshire accent with its flat vowels and hard consonants, and a rich vocabulary which eventually evolved, with English, Latin and Gaelic assistance, into the proud northern dialects. In Iceland, however, isolated in and insulated by the mighty Atlantic, the language retained its purity. The Icelanders still speak the language of the sagas and can read the centuries-old texts as we would read a modern novel. The language of the Vikings, Old Norse, is alive and well and living in Iceland.

But the Vikings left us much more than the heritage of language, they left us their blood. Even now, throughout the north, despite the intermingling of genes, the nordic traits appear in the blue eyes, the fair skin and the lighter tints of hair.

*   *   *

My early years were spent in Hindley, a small town of little consequence between Leigh and Wigan, barely big enough to warrant an Urban District Council. We were what people call *working class*, whatever that may mean. Adjacent to the family seat was a small brook decorated with deceased prams, redundant house-bricks and ancient bicycle parts, its wetness, and hence mine, being oft the cause of matriarchal wrath. This waterway was populated by loach, small and cat-fish-like, which mouthed sadly through the sides of jam-jars. There were water-boatmen and pond-skaters and swimming spiders, and it went to the sea, presumably at Blackpool for that was where the sea had its being. The name of this aquatic thoroughfare was Borsdane Brook, and it came from an even greater wonderland called Borsdane Wood. As I grew I came to know that wood as well as one can ever know anything. I knew its denizens from the humble water-vole to the magnificent tawny owl, and learned, from close observation, the mating habits of the weaver and the miner.

There was a day during my infancy when a square, polished box made an appearance in the home, its face a confusing array of fretwork, dials and knobs. This my grandad called a *wireless*. From it came sounds of crackling interspersed with snatches of the human voice, a strange voice speaking outlandish words in an almost totally unintelligible manner similar to the people on cinema screens. Thus it was that I learned to understand the English language, though I did not learn to *speak* it with any degree of success until Her Majesty required my presence in her brown-suited legions.

I came to learn that my native speech, in both vocabulary and accent, was confined to a very small area indeed and began to mellow into English the further from Hindley I went. Even in Wigan and Bolton there was a rounding of the flat vowels, and a softening of the hard, dental *t* which I pronounced like a *d*. Further afield the *dialect* became lost, merely the accent, the dropped *h* and the glottal-stop remaining to add flavour to the spoken English. It was also intriguing to discover that my own language could not successfully be written down in Roman script which lacked the range of my Hindley vowels.

When I travelled to the south, to Birmingham and remote regions beyond, everyone assumed me to be from Yorkshire. This was a cause of great trauma since, as every northerner knows, peace in the Wars of the Roses has never been declared by the people. In Yorkshire, too, I was assumed to be from another Riding; never from Lancashire.

A great thing is made of Yorkshire's Viking heritage. The Danelaw of Guthrum had its seat at York, then known as Jorvik, from where he administered the north and east of England, leaving the rest for Alfred the not-so-Great. But in Hindley and district there was silence. There was no digging. There were no known fortifications. There is no academic interest in the area. The only evidence for Viking settlement lies in the language, and in place names, and in the people themselves. I thought and dreamed long and hard of wing-helmeted warriors wielding their short swords in Bors*dane* wood; of Viking and non-Viking blood turning red the waters of Bors*dane* brook.

In the wood a friend discovered an ancient short sword, its blade ferrous and eaten but its gleaming brass handle in fine condition. It was hidden, and hoarded, and believed to be Viking. Occasionally it would be ritually shown, like some relic of religion, a primal link with heritage; then it would be reverently secreted lest those who did not understand should seek to take it away.

So it was that my yearning for heritage began. Gradually, as the years gathered, Iceland gained ascendancy over mainland Scandinavia as the object of my desires. The language and blood of Vikings no longer maintained their purity in Norway, Sweden or Denmark. They had become as mongrel as I. But in

Iceland still there was some degree of purity, close enough for me to feel kinship and to desire a meeting.

Ah, but a meeting with the people was not enough. My thoughts went towards the land which lured their free spirits; the harsh land, the fire land, the ice land. Gently the idea formed that I would experience a little of what they had experienced, they who came to that new land, who explored its secret places and made it their land. To go as a tourist, casually to see what they had seen, was not enough. There must be a challenge, a genuine quest the equal of their own. In Iceland there were many challenges for the adventurous, but one challenge seemed to stand supreme. It became evident, during my researches, that a crossing on foot from coast to coast along the island's east–west axis and through its interior had, in all probability, never been accomplished. Certainly such a journey had never been reported. The concept of accomplishing this journey *alone* began to form, making finger-ends tingle and scalp itch with excitement. I obtained large-scale maps and perused them in detail, thrilling at the obstacles of lava desert, volcano, black sand desert and glacier along the route. I studied the logistics of such a journey and, with some trepidation, pronounced it difficult, but just about feasible.

I decided to make the journey from Seyðisfjörður, a fjord harbour on the eastern coast with easy access by road, to Reykjavik the capital city in the west, using for the most part natural valley routes, crossing on the way the world's biggest lava desert of Mývatnsöraefi and the great black sand desert of Sprengisandur. If circumstances permitted I would make slight detours to cross the mighty glacier of Hofsjökull, to climb the active volcano of Hekla and to visit the Gullfoss waterfall and the hot springs of Geysir.

My journey was to be from east to west since the international airport, Keflavik, was on the west coast near the capital and I wished to be sure of catching my plane home on my Apex ticket which was valid for but four weeks. To be stuck on the wrong side of the island at check-in time would not be desirable. The penalty for this decision was that the powerful prevailing wind would be blowing into my teeth for the entire journey, not a pleasant prospect. This would be a formidable and arduous journey, but an appropriate challenge and a fitting way to make my acquaintance of Iceland, the land and the people. Yes, this was the way to encounter heritage; not only as a scholar, with the mind, but as a warrior, with the body and the soul. I would fight the wild island, and expect no quarter.

I thought of these things as Iceland came closer, as the dark North Atlantic sped beneath; and the blood of Vikings long dead stirred within me as the longship of the air grounded at Keflavik airport.

It was cold, wet, windy and eleven at night as I walked from plane to terminal. My rucksack carouselled into view, gleaming new ice-axe strapped to the back partly obscuring the Union Jack and the legend *Edwards Trans-Icelandic Expedition 1984*. I heaved and grunted it through the immigration department where a stern-faced lady demanded, 'Are you alone? . . . Have you a return ticket? . . . Show me your return ticket!' Officially joyless she bade me welcome to Iceland, returned my documents and commenced the litany and responses with the next passenger. 'Are you alone? . . .'

Thankfully the customs officials did not wish me to unpack what had taken over an hour to pack and I was soon aboard a coach on the half-hour journey to Reykjavik on the west coast. The rain lashed the wind-screen and was cleanly and very briefly removed by the wipers. Moorland whipped past, bleak and forbidding, with an occasional single-storey dwelling. Buildings all appeared new and temporary, an observation which was to gather strength during the following weeks.

We arrived at the Reykjavik terminal at the edge of a domestic airport, a massive glass and concrete edifice of a hotel which seemed to have designs upon my wallet. The rain had temporarily stopped so I left the hotel lights in search of a secluded patch of grass upon which to lay my travel-weary frame. This I found without difficulty and within a very few minutes had erected my hooped bivi, a one-man tent-cum-sleeping-bag-cover which I was testing for Survival Aids, a leading out-door equipment supplier and one of my sponsors. As soon as I had made myself comfortable and waterproof the rain began again, bashing the Gore-tex skin of the bivi like a kettle drummer. Consciousness drained away as I and the soil of Iceland blended together in a compromise of comfort.

The celestial percussionist began once more to batter my aural sensibilities as I emerged from insulating sleep. *Where am I? Ah yes! What is today's plan?* My first problem was that I was at the wrong end of the island. In twenty-seven days' time I had to be here at this place to commence my journey home. There was no time at all to lose. I must find transport along the coast to the east of Iceland without delay, but first I must attend to my innards which were complaining of lack of sustenance. I had eaten little the previous day, having been on the move for most of it. I was also beginning to feel the effects of my *wake* of the evening previous to my departure. The *wake* is a tradition borrowed from the Irish whereby the dear departed is placed in the room, coffin and all, and raucously lamented at great length with the aid of much alcohol. Since I hate to miss a good *wake*, and there was a great probability of my body remaining undiscovered in the event of my distant demise, I had opted to hold the wake prior to departure. The celebrations had continued into the lunch-time session of farewells, and now had come the time of reckoning.

The rain obligingly stopped and I unzipped myself into the Icelandic morning. Tall wet grass surrounded me, droplets clinging crystal-clear to the blades. The sky was the grey northern sky of home and a chill breeze blew. I packed up my camp and walked the quarter-mile or so to the hotel, which had a travel information desk and a cafeteria. Everyone spoke English; perfect southern English, but with the flat vowels of the north, like Lancashire union officials on TV interviews.

There was a bus for Höfn that very day, and within the hour. This would take the whole day and upon the morrow I could go from there to Egilsstaðir, a mere sixteen miles from my ultimate destination, the coastal town and port of Seyðisfjörður. This was lucky as in Iceland bus timetables are more concerned with days of the week than minutes of the day. I had time for breakfast so I strolled across the sumptuous carpet, leaving the patterned imprints of walking boots in my wake. From the cafeteria shelves I took a cheese roll and a sort of flat, square Eccles cake. A cup of tea seemed a good idea to flatten the fur on my tongue.

'One-hundred-and-twelve kronur please,' said the till lady. I fumbled with the unfamiliar currency and sat at a plastic-topped table. *One-hundred-and-twelve kronur?* At forty kronur to the pound that was almost three quid. The fur on my tongue seemed to grow a little.

The tea was of the continental variety; a tea-bag on a string lounging in comparative safety immersed in luke-warm water. I squeezed and kneaded it with my spoon, managing to produce a transparent grey fluid which became even more insipid with the addition of milk and sugar. I rubbed at the fur on my tongue with the cheese roll.

The Höfn coach was tall on massive tyres. I gratefully stowed my rucksack in the luggage compartment below and gained a left-hand window seat which would enable me to see inland throughout the day's journey and keep the sun out of my eyes. Eight-hundred-and-fifty kronur poorer after conducting business with the driver, I sat and watched Reykjavik roll away, a sprawling town with each building set in grounds, speaking of cheap land prices. There seemed little of architectural note save for some interesting modern churches with spires like inverted tin-tacks poking the sky.

Buildings became scarcer and gave way to very green grass; Irish green, lush green, wet green. Thick clouds were low, chopping off the tops of hills. Moss and lichen clung to rocks. A strange type of terrain came into view; great formlessly sculptured columns of some kind of rock covered with moss and seeming very difficult indeed to traverse. My map called it *stratified lava*. I knew that on my planned route there would be much of this. Horned, creamy, thick-wooled sheep watched us pass, unconcerned about anything but the taste of grass. Everywhere pylons strode the land going to and from various hydroelectric plants. Moorland began to dominate, soggy and boggy. Were there no trees in Iceland? Cows there were, and short hardy-looking ponies, but no trees. This, I reflected, could be a problem. All my food was freeze-dried and required boiling water to reconstitute it. Always on my expeditions of the past, even in the Sahara, there had been fuel to be found with which to light a fire. Here there seemed to be none. I had a little solid fuel for emergency use, but had considered the extra weight of a liquid- or gas-fuelled stove to be impractical for such an extended journey. Yes, here could be a problem.

Eastward we went down Route One, the main road which ringed the entire island. It was still early when we crossed the narrow, but by Icelandic standards great, bridge at Selfoss over the churning meltwaters of the mighty inland glaciers, brown, murky and powerful. On the quiet coach radio someone from long ago sang, '*Night and day, you are the one. Only you beneath the moon and under the sun . . .*' There was no smoking allowed on the coach. Everyone, despite multifarious origins, communicated with fellow passengers in English. '*In the roaring traffic's boom, in the silence of my lonely room, I think of you, night and day.*'

At around midday we ran out of road surface. From there

onwards Route One became a cinder track, what might be expected to lead to a remote hill farm and cease amid flapping ducks. From rocky shelves to my left dropped exquisite water-falls, straight and true like new-combed hair. Occasionally a cluster of two or three farms would proclaim brave human occupation of the land. The total population of Iceland is about 180,000, slightly higher than Salford, and mostly concentrated around Reykjavik.

In the afternoon the sun shone a little and we encountered the various snouts of Vatnajökull, supposedly Europe's largest glacier, a strange claim since it is on an island about two hundred miles from Greenland. No doubtful claims were necessary for the magnificently beautiful spectacle of those giant rivers of ice flowing at a sedate and indiscernible pace, terminating in great white walls which melted as fast as they advanced and rushed, liquid and joyous, home to the sea. As the sun dipped down the coach stopped at an iceberg factory, Lake Jökulsárlón, where bergs calved from the ice-wall and, transparently aglow with inner brilliance, performed a perpet-ual ballet of water and light. Could this be on the same planet that twenty-four hours earlier had boasted a grey railway station full of grey people on grey errands?

Höfn was a hotel and some houses. I paid seven pounds for an unspectacular meal of cold lamb, roast potatoes, salad and soup, strolled for a few minutes around the settlement, and slept on the grass of the idyllic shore far from the official camp-site of noise, bother and disturbance.

'There is no bus to Seyðisfjörður until tomorrow,' said the blonde goddess at the Egilsstaðir hotel where the bus ended its uneventful journey the following afternoon. I wished to spend that night on the east coast and start the trek westward the following morning. Whilst I considered my next move I obtained some money at the bank and indulged in the luxury of a tenner'sworth of lamb cutlets, justifying the extravagance by contemplating the weeks of culinary bleakness in prospect.

Since Seyðisfjörður was but sixteen miles distant I decided to hitch, so, loins suitably girded, I headed for the coastal hills which had to be crossed before the coast could be sighted. Seventy-two pounds was a heavy weight on level ground for one somewhat overweight whose principal exercise for over a year had consisted of raising glass containers a foot or so from elbow height. To heave that load two thousand feet up an incline which seemed at times to approach the vertical could only be described as an intense course in character-building. Frequent rests and heaving lungs were the order of the day as Egilsstaðir became smaller and lower. Traffic was quite frequent and very reluctant to stop as to do so would be to lose the momentum necessary to complete the climb with ease. My mood was resignedly philosophical as I neared the top, was picked up by a couple in a saloon car, and flopped gasping and red-faced into the back seat. I am not a fitness fanatic and never train physically for an expedition, being of the opinion that since the human body is basically a machine subject to all the problems of machines, then there is a finite amount of mileage in a pair of legs, and I have never had any intention of wasting that mileage pounding around familiar streets. I have always found that my body very quickly adapts to whatever situation it finds itself in, after an initial period of shock. This system I call my *baptism of fire principle*, and whilst it gives a little initial pain it does not appear to be dangerous like the methods advocated by 'fitness' freaks who annually die in their thousands or so often reach old age as bent and worn-out travesties of humanity.

Seyðisfjörður, a town of a thousand souls, its coloured houses scattered like churchyard confetti, sat amidst green at the end of its fjord. The car descended into it and dropped me at a petrol station which also served as a snack-bar and corner shop. I partook of a hot-dog and a coke for a couple of quid and set off down the fjord's northern shore for a spot from where I could see the open sea, the point where I felt that I could legitimately claim to be on the east coast of Iceland. Half an hour later I was there. The fjord swung around to the right, snow-topped hills dropping in green concave slopes to tuck their feet beneath the cool waters; and beyond the fjord a horizon geometrically flat, the Arctic Ocean, clear and unbroken to the Viking mainland six hundred miles distant. I had come to the beginning.

There is, the night before commencing an action wherein lies danger, a quiet time. It is a time of reflection and taking of stock. Danger is impossible to quantify. The same occurrence could bring a grazed knee or death, and in death there is no degree. In desert waste, on mountain ice or in one's own main street the final visitation is the same. All one can do is to be as prepared as one feels is necessary to meet whatever one expects, but all too often comes the unexpected.

It is then that the Angel of Death wings close, poised to snatch the soul. We were well acquainted, that angel and I; such old enemies that we were almost friends. *Old Baldie*, I called him, with his lipless grin and eyeless gaze. I had great respect for Old Baldie for he was a trier, and we both knew that one day he would not go back alone.

As the sun dipped behind the hills I ticked off in my mind each stage of the journey and catalogued my preparedness.

'There is moorland beyond Egilsstaðir and before Reykjavik. I know about moorland. For as long as I can remember I have travelled moorland. To the newcomer moorland can be a killer, but I know the ways of the moors; the bogs, the mists and the clouds. I have proper respect for the moors. Good clothing I have to keep out the weather, no matter how cold and wet, and map and compasses to guide me, no matter how bad the visibility. Yes, I am happy about the moorland.

'There will be rivers, deep and violent. Here could lie a major

danger. Swollen rivers are always greater killers than they seem. I have resolved that no heroics will be wasted on the rivers. If I judge the danger to be great then I will travel to safer crossings, to bridges, or even take passage by vehicle. Sound judgement will be my keeper. Yes, I am happy about the rivers.

'There are to be lava deserts. One is said to be the world's biggest, where Apollo astronauts trained before their moon landings. I have never crossed stratified lava. The only stratified lava I have ever seen was from the window of the bus near Reykjavik. It looked difficult. It looked like terrain where a man could break an ankle. To a man alone, in a place where other men do not go, a broken ankle could be a sentence of death. If the difficulty seems too great then I will go around it. I have only twenty-five days left before I must be in Reykjavik. About the lava deserts I am apprehensive, but on the whole, happy.

'The great sand desert of Sprengisandur stretches over a hundred miles through the centre of Iceland. A wasteland of black volcanic sand with violent sand-storms lashing against my direction of travel. I know about deserts for did I not conquer the Saharan Empty Quarter alone but last year? Three-hundred-and-fifty miles of waterless waste. On Sprengisandur there will be water. Probably there will be too much water. It will be physically and mentally demanding, but about the desert I am happy.

'At the centre of Sprengisandur is Hofsjökull, over twenty miles of glacier, its summit in excess of five thousand feet above sea level. Twenty miles of frozen water moving uncontrollably and unpredictably; crevasses, smooth-sided and deep, from which it is a rare thing to escape should one plunge into their depths. This is new to me. I have read the books. All my life I have read of the great glaciers of the Alps, of the polar ice caps, and of the mighty Rongbuk Glacier of Everest. Many good and experienced men have lost their lives to glaciers. I know the theory. I have read again the books. The equipment is here, cool and hard in my grasp. There is, about this tackling of a glacier alone and without practical experience, a little madness, but in life one must have a little madness or one could not leave the safety of the known and make progress. Yes, there is an element of pure gamble in *this, with death for the loser and achievement for the victorious. With proper caution in the execution of the attempt the odds are, I think, in my favour. But I must not be stupid! Old Baldie dances attendance upon the stupid. If, when I see the problem, it seems too great, then as I shall with the rivers, I will turn back. There will be no foolhardiness, but always sound and well-thought-out judgement. Accepting the now creeping fear of the unknown, about the glacier I am tentatively happy.*

'Finally there is Hekla, the horrendous active volcano, still smouldering from its eruption in 1981, three years ago. This, too, is new to me. What will it be like to climb the slopes to its smoking crater four and a half thousand feet in the sky? I do not know. I have no parameters. But others have climbed it; an estimated ten people each year look into the sulphurous depths, and so shall I. Yes, about the volcano I am happy.'

Before I left England someone from the press asked me if this was to be the first solo walk across Iceland. I replied that I didn't *know* it to be so, but that I would not be surprised to learn that it was. Such considerations seemed unimportant as I lay in my bivi on the eastern shore, my mind full of tomorrows, for no matter who had gone before, it was *my* first crossing. That was the thought uppermost as the day slipped from me into memory.

2 The Moor

The gale shook me awake at about three o'clock, flinging the rain remorselessly at my little haven of dryness. Sleep was spasmodic after this as the wind tried to blow me from my moorings and the rain attempted to wash this invader into the fjord. The hours ticked by ... four o'clock ... five o'clock ... six o'clock ... seven o'clock ... Still the elements raged. At half past seven there was a lull as both wind and rain subsided. Not knowing how long this respite would last I flung myself into the cold, newly washed morning. On and above the fjord seagulls argued the price of fish and, grey-backed, performed impossible aerobatics inches from the rippled waters. Rapidly I shook the surface water from my shelter and packed my camp into my rucksack; then, almost before I realised it, and without any ceremony, I began the great trek west.

Within half an hour I was at the centre of Seyðisfjörður's sparse dwellings from which people were beginning to emerge. They smiled friendly smiles and went about their business. No litter blew about the buildings in the cold morning breeze; neither crisp-packet nor coke-can, toffee-paper nor cigarette-packet, for they are a house-proud people, my northern cousins. The filling-station café was open so, just as the rain recommenced and the wind rose, I entered for breakfast.

A pleasant young girl, pretty because of her youth, served me a hot-dog and livening black coffee as the rain battered the large windows. I was the only customer and the girl had difficulty with English so I watched the rain-laden clouds churn above the coastal hills which were my first problem, and waited for a break in the weather. From time to time another customer would leap out of a car for the door clutching handfuls of empty coke bottles which were presented in part-exchange for full ones. I saw few drink cans in Iceland. One made an initial investment in a quantity of bottles, each bottle having a greater value than its contents, and henceforward treated these bottles as negotiable currency. The result was a saving in resources and no empty cans blowing about. Simple, really.

The stopping of the rain coincided conveniently with the demise of my hot-dog so, heaving my great rucksack upon my shoulders, I waved goodbye to the smiling girl and left the café on legs aching from the previous day's exertions. At the road junction a yellow sign designated the road to my right as Route 93 for Egilsstaðir and down it I went, feeling the weight on my back becoming heavier with each step. For a mile or so the road was level and pleasant to walk along. The sky was Salford-grey but the clouds were higher than the moor-green hilltops piebald with snow. The road began to mount the lower slopes and became steeper at every footfall. Seyðisfjörður shrank back to confetti as the east coast gradually receded. Once I looked back as I sat on a roadside rock to rest, and both town and coast were gone, hidden amongst the hills. I was alone and, despite the man-made road which led to men, felt incredibly remote.

I felt the rock on which I sat. It was solid and old; the oldest rock of Iceland excreted from the earth some sixteen million years ago during the Tertiary period and shoved outwards by the newer lava which belched even yet from the island's central area. It was difficult to think of sixteen million years ago as quite recent, but in geological terms indeed it was. Strata several feet thick, each from some antediluvian eruption, were clearly visible giving the basalt mountains the aspect of mighty cream-topped gâteaux.

A stream bounced beside the road and occasionally I would

drink its crystal waters, devoid of purifying impurities. Sometimes it would fall over a rock shelf or squeeze itself through a deep cleft, mumbling to itself at the inconvenience. The world was pleasing and my journey unhurried, and happily the rain and gale rested awhile. By mid-morning I was at the top of the pass and the road began to curve downwards, at first tentatively with an occasional uphill stretch, but before long it made up its mind and homed in on the valley below. I passed the point where the previous day I had obtained my lift, and continued over the now familiar ground wondering why I had thought the road so steep on the way up. Egilsstaðir came into view, seeming small and insignificant with the great wide Lagarfljót river behind, and beyond that rose the moor made blue-green by distance and extending over the horizon. This was to be my first challenge.

It began to rain as I passed through the outskirts of the town. Few people were about, and those few milled around the entrance to a new modern supermarket clutching plastic bags of shopping or pushing prams laden with goods and blond children. All were dressed in quilted anoraks, woolly hats and scarves against the North Atlantic weather. The supermarket car park was filled with cross-country vehicles; German Hefflingers, Japanese Toyotas, American Fords and British Land Rovers. A further international flavour was given by the flags of many nations which flew from flag-poles before the supermarket as before a convention of world commerce, as I suppose it was.

The rain began to fall steadily, running down litterless gutters. There is nothing that the weather can manifest which is quite so misery-provoking as the onset of rain. Great storms can stir the blood; but rain, aimless and casual, is just dreary. Entering a café I expended enormous resources on a square meal of lamb cutlets. I ordered a tea and watched, mesmerised, as the resident Valkyrie opened a thermos flask and poured water onto a perfectly innocent tea-bag. A little cloud of sad steam hung lazily close to the surface like early morning mist, and was gone.

'Have you no *boiling* water?' I asked politely, and not unreasonably. The Valkyrie thought for a moment, her brows wrinkling with concentration as she attempted to understand the implication of my question. She spoke.

'This *is* boiling water,' she said in tones conveying her lack of comprehension. The tea-bag remained clearly visible through the crystal liquid. I poked an experimental finger into the cup.

'No, this is *warm* water,' I explained. Again her brows furrowed.

'Does it matter?' she asked, in genuine innocent enquiry.

'Yes!' I almost shouted. 'It matters very much!'

She dutifully went away, shaking her head, to boil some water, unaware of the depth of the great revelation which had been laid at her feet. Minutes later she returned with a steaming pan and scalded another tea-bag. She looked in amazement as the water became a deep amber. Then a smile of understanding spread over her face as she realised that the tea-bag had a purpose other than as a ritual object.

In Iceland it is the custom that when one buys a cup of tea one may continue to pour water upon the tea-bag for subsequent cups free of charge. As I approached the counter for my second, third and fourth cup my protégée would vanish into the kitchen and gleefully reappear with the steaming pan to repeat the demonstration of her brand-new culinary skill.

It was late in the afternoon when the rain stopped. There was still time to make it onto the moor, so heaving my great burden onto my protesting body I set off for the river. I passed houses, shops, filling-stations and banks. Every building in Iceland seemed shy of its neighbour, built outward instead of upward and set behind huge lawns and forecourts. All was space with the horizon always visible between the structures.

And all was new and clean, as fresh and unpolluted as were the smiling people. I decided that I liked Iceland.

The wind howled as I crossed the long, narrow bridge over the Lagarfljót, the waters churning beneath the wooden pier-like roadway. I walked on down Route One for a couple of miles and left it behind as I trudged along a narrow lane towards the moor. There were intermittent showers to cool me down as the track led deeper into the Derbyshire-like grassland. A few creamy-white sheep watched my passage and from time to time I would encounter a small farm complete with tail-wagging guardian professionally barking. Fences were everywhere, tufts of wool clinging to the barbed wire and blowing in the constant wind. I passed a small family grave-plot fenced against irreverent animals. Here in this sparsely populated country one is not buried amongst strangers and one's connection with one's land continues even beyond death.

The track ended in a farmyard. Behind it, a stone wall and the steep slope of the open moor. I saw no-one as I walked around the side of the house, past a child's swing and a brightly coloured ball, and clambered over the wall. Here was the moor, springy-grassed and hummocky. The dead weight of my pack pushed me down into the ground as I began to tackle the slope. It was getting late and the light was fading. There seemed little chance that I would reach the top that day so my thoughts went towards a search for water near which to camp. I found a small stream in a sheltered gully with a flat patch of grass for my hooped bivi. Gratefully I snapped open my waist strap and eased the load to the ground. Within minutes my shelter was erected and sleeping-bag installed. It was now necessary to boil water in order to reconstitute a freeze-dried meal. There was no natural fuel about so I devised as much shelter as possible for my solid-fuel stove and placed a couple of the grey tablets on their platform.

For an hour I cosseted the stove's small flame against the wind and several tablets later the water was beginning to get hot. More tablets, but still it would not boil. Finally, rather than use up more of my meagre fuel supplies, I poured the quite hot water into the two packets, one containing chicken supreme and the other rice, stirred them around and left them to soak for a couple of minutes. The resulting meal was usually quite palatable, but because the water had not been hot enough what I got was a half-reconstituted luke-warm paste full of crunchy hard bits. It was a sign of my state of hunger that I ate the whole revolting mess.

As I ate, my limbs began to stiffen. Since morning I had walked twenty-five miles during which I had heaved my load up two thousand feet, down two thousand feet and up another thousand. The average daily distance that I was aiming for was twenty miles, so I reflected that this was probably the hardest day that there would be, considering the fact that as I moved over Iceland my load would become lighter and the terrain flatter. It was a satisfying thing to see the line that I drew on my map stretching substantially inland, but it had to be paid for in the draining of energy. I was utterly exhausted as my watch told me it was ten p.m. and the glow of the all-night sun silhouetted the next day's slopes. I slept a satisfied sleep to regain my strength for the morning's rigours.

So did Old Baldie!

At twenty-two minutes past six on the morning of the second day I became a hero. I leaped out of my nice warm sleeping-bag and plunged my bruised and throbbing feet into the freezing stream. Of such things are heart-attacks made. One must, at all times, keep one's feet clean when walking or cramps and all manner of pains will result. Soon the initial shock gave way to a welcome numbness as my toes turned an interesting shade of maroon. The wind had dropped so there was little trouble in breakfasting on beef curry, rice and tea. I did a little photography, both still and cine, and set about the heart-rending task of reducing my pack's weight. Parts of my body I had completely forgotten about were screaming abuse so something had to be done about that load.

Digging a shallow grave I laid to rest about five pounds of freeze-dried food, reasoning that since there didn't seem to be any natural fuel about and my solid fuel was strictly limited then much of it was useless to me. I had lived my life for the most part in a monetarist society, and to throw away over ten pounds' worth of goods hurt deeply, but out there on the moor money was valueless and money'sworth of even less use. I also interred half my toilet-roll and the first three-quarters of Tom Sharpe's *Indecent Exposure*, retaining the un-finished bit for emergency chuckles.

I filled my one-litre aluminium water-bottle, veteran and old friend of four Saharan expeditions, snapped the lid shut and watched with sadness as a thin stream of water spurted out from near the neck until the internal pressure dropped. A leaky water-bottle . . . just what I needed! This meant that I would be more dependent upon camping by streams. Still, I mused, it meant that I would have less weight to carry, which was all to the good.

There was a little surface mist still clinging to the hills as I turned towards the moor tops, my pack feeling very much lighter. Ahead was twenty miles of trackless moorland traversed by numerous streams and punctuated by areas of bog. Twenty miles to the west I would encounter a road which would take me a further thirty miles westward to a great river beyond which was my lava desert. The cloud thinned and the sun blazed from an egg-shell-blue sky. I rolled up my jeans and sleeves to let the quite strong breeze reach my body. A view of panoramic beauty presented itself behind me with the wide silver Lagarfljót river, really a long lake at that point, filling the valley, and beyond it the blue-grey coastal hills, one or two of obvious volcanic origin. It was beauty that needed to be captured on film.

I tried out a new mounting for taking pictures of myself. Since a tripod is cumbersome and extra weight, I had drilled a hole in the blade of my ice-axe to take a camera screw fitting with a universal joint. I fitted my still camera to the axe, rammed the point solidly into the earth, set up the shot and wound up the timer. When satisfied I prodded the timer button, ran to my appointed place on the landscape and sat gazing casually out over the vista posing like mad. Satisfied, I repeated the operation with the movie camera. Since I could carry only a small quantity of film each shot had to be meticulously prepared and every frame had to count. There could be no casual use of film in the hope that the law of averages would produce something good. Immortalising one's self on celluloid is a great consumer of time. It can take upwards of half an hour to produce twenty seconds of film. In terms of progress I always look upon time spent filming as an official rest period since it is mind more than body that is being utilised.

It was not long before I found myself on the moorland plateau. The wind was very strong from the south-west and I wished to go west to my next goal, a mile-long lake named Sandvatn which I estimated to be about two miles away. It was not that I particularly wished to see the lake but it would be the next recognisable feature along my route and when I found it I would know my exact position on the map. To check my position I took bearings with my compass on a couple of mountain summits, and upon drawing the appropriate lines on my map found that I was standing in the precise centre of the lake. 'Something is wrong,' I thought. I checked everything again, and yet again using another compass, with the same result. There could be but one explanation. Something in the ground, probably iron ore, was interfering with the compass needles and making them unreliable.

I wasn't unduly worried as visibility was excellent and I could tell my approximate whereabouts from the positions of the distant mountains with reference to my map. Westward I went and a little over an hour later found myself on the shores of Sandvatn, black, cold and forbidding, ringed by the black volcanic sand which gave it its name. My boots made Man Friday tracks on the sand's pristine surface. As I rested Arctic skuas walked close, fearless and inquisitive, unaware that man could be harmful. Around me was the landscape of the Pennines, but the horizon was that of Switzerland with jagged peaks clad in snow like the teeth of a mighty Alsatian.

There was a river to cross. I walked over to where it flowed into the lake and inspected it. It was about a hundred yards wide, quite slow-moving and seemed to get no deeper than a couple of feet. Not dangerous and no real problem, but since wet feet are not comfortable feet I walked upstream looking for a place to cross dry-shod. Such a place was quickly found with stepping-stones leading onto and beyond a small island. Choosing my route carefully I leaped from stone to stone like a ballet-dancing gibbon. As I was about to take off from a rock a massive greylag goose leaped honking from its hide about fifteen feet away and, flapping its enormous span of wings, dragged its huge bulk over the water's surface and into the blue sky. Startled, I lost my footing and my right foot shot from the rock, coming to rest on the river-bed well below the surface. Philosophically I felt the cold water rush through the boot-top and penetrate to every crevice not already occupied by foot or sock. Addressing the airborne banquet in most unflattering terms I blunderd my way to the far shore, removed the brimming boot and sodden sock, and wrung out as much water as possible.

It was then that I realised how nasty that little mishap could have been. The area may well have looked like my native Pennine moors, but these were *not* the Pennine moors. These were moors that few people ever visited. Probably no-one had been here for months, or even years, and it could be a similar time before anyone passed this way again; indeed, it was conceivable that no-one had *ever* been here. With the kind of weight I had on my back, what would normally be a sprained ankle could very easily be a broken one, and a broken ankle on a moor with no chance of rescue could well be a ticket to Old Baldie's lair. 'Don't stick your neck out Ted,' I told myself. 'Be careful . . . Be BLOODY careful!'

The ground had become flat and boggy with patches of cotton-topped plants like dandelion clocks bending in the strong wind. Very little of Iceland is covered by vegetation, and this is mostly near the coast. Because of its isolated position there are only about 400 species of stemmed plants as compared to the British total of over 2,300. Abundant, however, thanks to the constant dampness, are mosses, lichens and fungi with upwards of a thousand species, many yet to be catalogued. In the years of Iceland's early settlement it is recorded that extensive forests of birch clad the coastal plain, but deforestation and the action of sheep have caused them to retreat to a few sheltered valleys and plains. Thirty-foot birches are still the largest trees on the island, with a few yew-leafed willows and rowan trees scattered amongst them, but the only trees I saw in Iceland were a few stunted dwarf-birches in the lowlands.

I ascertained my direction by using the old boy-scout method of pointing the hour hand of my watch at the sun and dividing the angle between it and twelve. As the watch showed Greenwich Mean Time this gave me the direction of south. From this information it was a simple matter to estimate my direction of travel. There was a mountain on the horizon in that direction so I used it as my beacon, correlating it with my map. This method, though it may seem crude, is surprisingly accurate. Distance was estimated by first knowing my normal pace over reasonable terrain with a full pack.

Then I would take into account the roughness of the ground, the weight of my load and anything else that could affect my speed such as strong wind, physical condition and even my mood, and bearing in mind all of these factors make an educated guess at the distance covered in the given time. With practice it is possible to be absolutely spot-on with this method over a period of days.

My immediate destination was a road which crossed my line of march some fifteen miles from Sandvatn lake. Two hours after leaving its shores I topped a rise beyond which was a rocky drop of a hundred feet or so. The wind howled and battered, trying to throw me to the ground. Gratefully I dropped my pack and sat on a rock to rest. The sky was blue and cloudless still. I sucked a mint and drank a little water, pleased that very little had leaked from the hole in the bottle. The dog's tooth hills were clear on the horizon in all directions, except . . . Then I saw that they had gone from the south-west. A wall of low cloud was moving in with the wind, hugging the moor and coming in fast.

'It will be here within the hour,' said a voice, taunting, somewhere in my head. Old Baldie, everyone's bad penny, had finally turned up. The cloud looked pretty thick. I had to decide quickly whether to sit it out or try to get off the moor. I knew that low cloud could last for days and cooking in that wind was impossible. I had a little cheese and bread for emergency, but not enough for several days. My map told me that five miles to the north was a valley down which ran Route One. The edge of the plateau at its nearest point was three miles roughly in that direction. I decided to make for there. If I could reach the edge of the drop before visibility was blanked out then, with care, I should be able to reach the valley floor. There was a large triangular snow-field on a mountain about thirty miles to the north. Grabbing my rucksack I turned towards it, picking my way gingerly through the neat-edged basalt chunks on the downward drop with always the thought, 'Take care! . . . Take care! . . . Take care! . . .' to keep Old Baldie at bay.

A little over an hour later the cloud engulfed me. Within seconds visibility was reduced from over thirty miles to under thirty yards. It was cold with a dampness that seemed to seep through clothing and flesh and into bones to mix in with marrow. The triangle of snow was gone. I could not be much more than an hour from the moor's edge so I decided to go on, using the note of the wind in my left ear as a kind of sonar to keep me heading north.

The ground became hummocky so that I had to jump from one hummock to the next, a potentially dangerous procedure but under the circumstances probably less so than hanging about. Visibility dropped to twenty yards, and then to ten, and to five. Checking my sonar note I continued north on this boy-scout's nightmare, knowing that somewhere in that mist Old Baldie was pacing along with me, waiting for me to step over a hidden cliff or break a leg. To stay cheerful I talked into my tape-recorder, a small light-weight device kept in my breast pocket.

It seemed that very little else could go awry, but I was, of course, wrong. Old Baldie must have his little joke. There was an insistent churning of my innards the advent of which had but one meaning – *diarrhoea*! That crystal-clear stream of which I had partaken the previous evening and that morning must, at some stage, have passed through a sheep, either alive or dead. Now it was hell-bent on passing rapidly through me. It is difficult to feel intrepid when obtaining relief in those conditions. Later I continued north making a point of keeping up and down movement to an absolute minimum and footfalls as gentle as possible. A faint chuckle, I swear, came from somewhere nearby in the cloud.

I found a stream bouncing and gurgling down a shallow gully. It was like finding a highway. Descending the bank I followed it downhill, sliding on the moss and lichen-covered rocks. Its angle became steeper and the gully deeper. After a while I decided to walk along its rim in case it became too deep to exit from. The whole moor was now sloping gently and I knew I had reached the edge of the plateau.

Suddenly I was below the cloud and the valley was visible beneath me, the silver river wandering along its bottom. I checked its curves with the map and found myself to be exactly where I wanted to be, which, no matter how often I do it, always comes as a surprise. Leaving Old Baldie muttering and planning in the clouds I carried on downhill.

An hour later I was on the valley floor walking along a rough track with the river to my right. I was very tired indeed and hunger was beginning to make itself felt. If I had been in England there would have been, within a short distance, a friendly pub where one could eat pie and peas, or soup-in-the-basket, and imbibe vast quantities of foaming ale served with a genial smile by mein host who would discourse at length upon the pedigree of his whippets. However, this was not England, and the land of the Sagas where tales of Valhalla once rang through the valleys is now, to all intents and purposes, dry. Even a roadside café is a rare thing.

The wind rushed down the valley, much too strong to allow me to cook. I rested and ate my bread and cheese, then sucked my last Uncle Joe's Mint-ball to keep me all aglow. Route One was really the only practical route west from there, and Route One was on the other side of a river so wide, deep and fast that to consider crossing it other than by a bridge would have been utter madness. There was such a bridge an hour away so that was my next goal. It was a recent Meccano-like construction, temporary like every other bridge I had seen in Iceland, and as I crossed it, it began to rain. I had with me a Lionheart jacket donated by Survival Aids, who had supplied my bivi, and a pair of overtrousers. As the rain became insistent I donned my armour and carried on. Misery was paramount. The fact that I was dry and warm beneath the Gore-tex did little to relieve my mood. To tramp down an endless grey valley along a stony track with wind and rain going the other way and a huge pack on one's back; to do this for mile after mile after mile, with no change in the scenery and nothing to relieve the monotony, was not nice. There was neither magnificence of vista nor sense of progress to give meaning to my exertions. Crunch . . . crunch . . . crunch . . . crunch . . . crunch . . . crunch . . . crunch went my boots in perpetual rhythm . . . left . . . right . . . left . . . right . . . left . . . right . . . left. The only place to go to get away from this tedium was inward, so leaving my body to battle the elements, I retreated to the past.

The beat of the boots sent me back to the barrack square, to Kinmell Park, Rhyl, where as a raw recruit I was taught the all-important intricacies of drill by a new young minor god displaying a single chevron to denote his superiority to the majority and his inferiority within the pantheon. He would stand, ramrod-straight, and bellow some such arcane instruction as 'Squad will move to the right in threes! By the left . . . Quick . . . MARCH! . . . Eff! Eye! Eff! Eye! Eff! Eye! Eff!' We would dutifully stamp, twirl, slap rifles, wheel and flail arms about like demented windmills. Eventually we got our act together and at the passing-out parade, before the top brass, we marched past, thumbs uniformly straight and level with the shoulders. And we did this with pride, for though I have always been an individualist there is, I find, great dignity in absolute uniformity of action. Neither the action itself, nor its underlying purpose, matter in this respect. It is the uniformity of the action, be it a dance, a choral song, a war chant or the total humility of communal prayer that brings the pride, and as such helps to elevate the flagging individual to the level of magnificence of the whole.

I was dragged from my reverie by the sound of a diesel engine behind me. An articulated lorry bowled rapidly down the track, gave a loud blast of greeting on its horn, and roared, swaying, to the west. Ahead was a small collection of buildings. Could there be food to be had? As I approached the first house an elderly lady was tending the garden. I wished her a good afternoon and asked if there were a restaurant in the hamlet.

'There is no restaurant here. The next one is at Möðrudalur,' she beamed, in hesitant but perfect English.

'Is there a shop here?'

'No. In Möðrudalur.'

I thanked her and passed upon my way. Möðrudalur was twenty-eight miles away. I would not reach it that day. The wind laughed at me. Whilst it blew I could not use solid fuel and I had seen no natural fuel all day. Therefore the only usable food I had was half a small loaf, a minute piece of cheese and a few boiled sweets. Things were looking not too good, particularly since the next day was Sunday and the merchants of Möðrudalur, being doubtless good Lutherans, would not wish to profane the sabbath. But sufficient unto the day is the evil thereof. I would worry about that tomorrow. Right now the important thing was to move west, so onward I went down the stony track, eff, eye, eff, eye, eff, eye, eff!

My road began to slope steeply upwards and as the day aged I found myself high on the moorland again. The cloud cover thinned and evening sky became visible through the silver streaks. A stream ran under the road, deep in a gully, and there was a small flat area big enough to lie on. I set up camp and began to stiffen. On the road I found a wooden marker with a small reflector on top. It was about three feet long and broken at its base where some vehicle had ploughed into it. Never again would it be used for its intended purpose, but I had a brief future for it. It burned well under my pan and soon I was eating spicy beef and mashed potatoes, washing it down with hot, sweet tea. I was incredibly tired for that day I had covered, according to the map, over thirty miles. There was a raw patch on my right heel which required medical attention. The battle was over for day two. There was no time to reflect upon the day's events as I lay down and was immediately asleep.

The Vikings were not a nation, but a loose-knit collection of Scandinavian peoples. Scholars still argue about the origin of the name, but in essence a Viking was a knight of the sea with his own code and no worse than any other warrior of the Middle Ages. Yet this hotchpotch of independent, autonomous people assaulted the frontiers of art, gave the world a great literature and explored as far as Russia to the east and North America to the west. Wherever they went they were as much admired as feared and they left a legacy which still stirs the hearts of free men. Early in the seventh century a population explosion around the Scandinavian trade route known as *Norvegur*, the North Way, caused the people to settle in more inhospitable parts of the land. This pressure became more intense and burdensome as the eighth century came, with political pressures caused by the advent of aspiring royal houses.

Coincidentally the technology of northern naval architecture gave birth to the longship, the finest seagoing craft the world had ever seen. It was swift and sleek, powered by a great square sail and rows of oars. Big enough, it was, to carry a raiding party and return with booty. The young men, brave with the blood of youth, raided the coasts of Scandinavia and Europe to augment their meagre resources. The bravest went over the western sea to discover the Hebrides, the Shetlands and the Faroes. On the 8th of June 793 Anno Domini they made a raid on the Benedictine priory on the Holy Island of Lindisfarne, just off the Northumbrian mainland, and thus began the Viking era in Britain.

Where the raiders pioneered, the settlers followed. They came in the heavy *knörr* cargo ships with their families and their livestock, and the spirit of freedom came with them.

So it was that in the year AD 860 the longship of one Naddod, bound for the settlement of Faroe, was blown off-course
by a storm. When the winds abated he found himself south of
a land of glaciers and snows. He was not impressed. However, when he finally made landfall in the Faroes he spread the
word of the land he called *Snowland*. About the same time a
Swede named Gardar Svavarsson was heading for the Hebrides when he, too, was blown to this land of snows. He
landed to investigate, then westward along the south coast he
steered, around the western shores and to the inhospitable
northern ice. There he was forced to winter. In spring he
completed his circumnavigation, ascertaining thereby that
this land was an island, and continued on his interrupted
journey to the Hebrides where he, too, told his tale.

Word spread and two years or so later a Norwegian named
Floki left Norway with wife, children and cattle, and sailed for
Shetland and the Faroes. From there he set out for this land of
which he had been told. With him he had three caged ravens,
which is why he is known to history as Raven Floki. He was
not sure of the island's distance, and had only a vague idea of
its direction, so the ravens were to be his scouts. When the
Faroes dropped beyond his horizon he released one of the
ravens. Up it flew and from its exalted position saw its Faroe
home to which it happily returned. Later, when he let another
go, it circled for a while but, seeing no land, returned very
sensibly to the ship. Noah, it would seem, had similar problems.

Then one day he released the bird again. It flew up, then
vanished to the west. Floki followed and landed roughly
where had Gardar before him. For two years he struggled for
survival, but he was a better ornithologist than a farmer and at
the demise of his last cow he returned with his tale of woe. He
it was who gave the island the name of Iceland.

A few years after Floki's excursion a despot by the name of
Harald Fine-hair attempted to unite all Norway beneath his

kingship. Many fled west and one such, a chieftain named Ingolf who had particularly angered Harald, sailed out for Iceland. When in sight of its shores he took the ornately carved pillars of his high-seat, a kind of throne, and flung them into the sea. Ingolf worshipped Thor the god of thunder and war, to whom the pillars had been consecrated, and swore that he would build his settlement where they came ashore. Now Thor, it seems, held Ingolf in great regard for the pillars floated ashore in the best harbour on the island. It was sheltered and the geothermal activity in the area gave it the obvious name of Smoky Bay which, in Old Norse, is *Reykjavik*.

There Ingolf stayed, and prospered. When it became known that Iceland was habitable there was a land-rush from all the northern settlements where Harald had mounted punitive raids. From the Shetland, Faroe and Hebridean islands they came; from Ireland, England, Scotland and the island kingdom of Mann they sailed, bringing their brown-haired Celtic brides. Sixty years after Naddod was blown off-course there were twenty thousand free souls in Iceland, farming, fishing and laying the foundations for the next generations. Ten years later, in 930, these free people who wanted naught of kings set up the Iceland Free State, a republic ruled by the *Althing*, the world's first true parliament, almost three hundred years before the Magna Carta was sealed at Runnymede.

At times during the night I was aware that it was raining heavily. I arose during an early morning respite, made my feet mauve in the stream and set off down the road as the rain began again, breakfasting on stale bread and cheese as I walked. The moor had been replaced by black slag with great volcanic slag-heaps stark against the sky. These were long-dead Plio-Pleistocene volcanoes, which means that they erupted just over one and a half million years ago, belching from the Earth's bowels and pushing the older coastal rocks towards the sea. Little rain channels were written through the utterly barren land, dead with the absolute death of the stillborn. It was country that I knew well for I had grown up in such surroundings in my native Lancashire. I picked up a handful of the dead earth. It was the same stuff. Black, damp, cloying waste mixed with sharp grit forever devoid of life. Even in the world's great sand deserts there was not such desolation. This was a natural landscape, but we of Lancashire had had to make our own, to dig it from the earth and bring it, with the useful coal, up the impossibly deep mine-shafts, to discard it in great imposing heaps which were spread by rain and wind over the land. Some heaps we built from iron and steel slag, the useless scum of the furnaces. Many years I had spent building those dead heaps with the flesh and blood of dead men in labour totally devoid of dignity.

The rain stopped and the sky became cloudily blue, a canopy of beauty above the ugliness beneath. I descended into a green valley with a great wide and silver river flowing north to the sea. This was the mighty River Jökulsá á Fjöllum filled with the meltwaters of Vatnajökull glacier. Somehow I had to cross that river to the lava desert beyond. And there too sat Herðubreið, the steep-sided and flat-topped birthday-cake of a mountain, a single candle for a peak at its centre and icing dribbling down towards the lava plain five thousand feet below. Herðubreið was to dominate my horizon for many days to come.

Around noon I entered Möðrudalur; a house, a small neat church and a hut of a café, all painted brilliant white and lorded over by a shiny red Coca-Cola sign. The only life was a small ginger dog, friendly and happy, barking in greeting rather than in warning. Sheep grazed beyond fences of barbed-wire, their wooden posts leaning at odd angles. It was Sunday and the people would doubtless be in the church, or perhaps visiting elsewhere. They were not to be seen in

Möðrudalur. Nothing seemed to be cultivated; neither grain nor root-crop. No ploughs stood in barns, no hoes in sheds, no tractors in yards. This was sheep country, the meadow-grass clinging to life in the silt of the river. There seemed little point in staying so I continued down the road.

I had harboured thoughts of striking out over the fields towards the river at this point as I wished to start my crossing of the lava desert just beyond it, a paltry seven miles away. Unfortunately the fields were largely bog and water-meadow, not the most practical of terrain to traverse. I doubted if it would be a practical idea to attempt a crossing of the river anyway, having seen its width from above the valley. There was a bridge some twenty miles to the north along the road so I decided to head for it, keeping an eye open for any crossing opportunity which might present itself en route.

Still the wind howled. The afternoon sky became grey once more and the rain, a streaky grey curtain hanging in the west, came closer and engulfed me. It was time for some decisions. There was seemingly no possibility of heating water in these conditions with my equipment. If I couldn't heat water then I couldn't eat at all as I had finished my bread and cheese. There was nowhere ahead on my route to obtain food, and from the evidence of the last few days there was precious little chance of finding natural fuel. I would therefore have to go to where I could obtain either food that needed no reconstituting, or acquire a better stove. About this I had little choice. I had made some wrong assumptions in my planning and they must be corrected. My nearest town was Egilsstaðir where I had been two days previously. I must return there as quickly as possible to reequip.

From time to time a vehicle would race down the track. That day there had been two or three. I resolved to try for a lift from the next one going east. Things happened quickly then. A van came along and stopped. The driver said he would take me to Egilsstaðir and I piled into the back. Then off we went, bouncing over the hard-won miles back to civilisation. I knew that this was not a giving-up, but merely a strategic withdrawal; still there was in my mind the thought that this was so often a euphemism for *defeat*. It left a nasty taste in the mouth as the van lurched eastward down Route One's rutted road.

3 The Slag

Reindeer and chips with peas and carrots, followed by tea meticulously made with boiling water, are fine things to raise the spirits. Once, some Christmases previously, I had been Father Christmas, complete with grotto and plastic reindeer, in a local store. I was sure that those wide-eyed children, whose secrets I had shared, would not have approved of the way I gleefully attacked the dead beast. The tea-valkyrie was welcoming and performed her new tea-trick.

As I left the Egilsstaðir café the night was becoming cold. There were noises and general goings-on at the official camp-site so I set up camp outside of town and slept the smiling sleep of well-being. The night was quite calm, as was the morning. Locating the supermarket I made for the camping section looking for a suitable stove. There wasn't one. The only stoves they had were of the gas cartridge variety which were almost as useless in the wind as was solid fuel. I bought bread, biscuits, sardines, vacuum-packed salami and chocolate, sufficient for a meagre diet for seven days, considering that in at least some places ahead I would be able to boil water. In the café I gorged myself on hot-dogs and a bottle of beer which proudly proclaimed itself to be non-alcoholic, thus bringing shame upon its German brewers.

I obtained transport back along Route One which called in at the now open Coca-Cola café at Möðrudalur. There I enquired about the possibility of crossing the river. The locals impressed upon me at great length the impossibility of such an endeavour. It is my wont to view the word *impossible* as a clarion-call to action for it usually means that the task is too difficult for the *speaker* to contemplate. I had, however, seen the river and on this occasion the trumpets did not sound. It may well have been possible, but the odds against gaining the far shore alive were mighty odds, not the kind of odds I like.

This, the magnificent Jökulsá á Fjöllum, was the mightiest river in Iceland. One hundred and twenty-eight miles long, it began its life as a hot spring beneath the Vatnajökull glacier to the south. Along its length were powerful rapids, great ravines and four waterfalls, one of which, Dettifoss, is said to be the greatest in Europe. A year previously the Iceland Breakthrough Expedition, led by Paul Vander-Molen of Britain, had explored the whole length of this river from the glacial ice-caves to the Arctic Ocean using kayaks for most of its waters and ferrying the boats by microlight aircraft over the suicidal sections, the first time this combination of vehicles had been used. They almost lost an expert canoeist in white water. I decided to walk to the bridge despite the fact that it meant a two-day detour to the north.

Five miles beyond Möðrudalur I left my transport and began to walk. The added weight of my new food was cripplingly heavy so to compensate I threw out more freeze-dried food. Happily the wind was resting and reduced to quite a pleasant breeze. The land was fenced and greenly pastoral, and white flocks of clouds trotted evenly through the pale blue sky. It was a gentle sort of a day; a Sunday, three-cornered sandwich sort of day; the sort of day when happenings are immanent but never manifest. I remembered such days as a child when, tired of waiting for things to happen, I would cause them to occur. School, and confinement therein, were not for such days. They were days for the climbing of trees and the catching of sticklebacks, days to tramp the wild Ince Moss with its swamps and shouting birds, days so brimming with adventure and discovery that the inevitable tutorial and parental wrath paled into comparative insignificance. Those were days when learning took place.

Early evening saw me entering the hamlet of Grimsstaðir.

My map told me that it owned a petrol station and an airfield. My hope had been that it also owned a café. The half-expected minimetropolis revealed itself to consist of two houses and a couple of fuel pumps. There was a white-haired old gentleman who smilingly confirmed that grim indeed were the prospects in Grimsstaðir. He offered me the hospitality of his field which I graciously declined for I was but three miles from the bridge and wished to cross it and view the mighty river before that night's slumber.

Route One moved sharply to the left just beyond the houses. This was the most northerly point of the entire trip; indeed it was the furthest north I had ever been, a mere sixty-two miles from the Arctic Circle. About me the lush green grass, the grazing sheep and the warm jewel of the sun gave the lie to schoolboy notions of Arctic wastes. An hour or so later two white pylons appeared in the distance. I thought it strange that there should be only two but supposed the rest of the series to be hidden amongst the distant black slag-heaps. A short time later I realised that they were the twin towers of a suspension bridge, two great white concrete *pi* signs stark against the volcanic black.

I heard the river before I saw it; a rushing, gurgling, roaring, sloshing white-noise of a sound that tingled the senses with the fear of nature's might. Then I saw it, brown and white-flecked, running headlong to Dettifoss Waterfall fifteen miles to the north and angry at the delay. The monumental bridge, its tense cables curved with mathematical beauty, shouted man's temporary defiance across nature's bastion. I passed the massive anchor points, the cables buried deep in heavy concrete, and walked the incongruous rutted dirt roadway across the churning waters beneath. At this, the narrowest local point of the river, it was 135 yards between the towers. Now this may not seem a great distance to anyone accustomed to the suspension bridges of Forth, Clifton or Humber, but it was probably the most substantial structure I saw in Iceland

and to see it isolated in the landscape, to be alone with its audacity and therefore to form a personal relationship with it, was a profound experience bordering upon the religious.

The sun was dipping. I had no wish to leave the bridge so I looked for a place to camp. The whole ground was covered in black volcanic sand fine enough to be called soot, and to walk upon its level virginity was to defile it. But defile it I did and pitched camp amongst some grass-topped dunes to shelter from the soft breeze.

Dried grass from the tops of the dunes formed my fire and I was soon tucking into a hot steaming supper with a mug of sweet tea to follow. At about midnight a slightly gibbous moon arose above the low eastern hills into an almost clear Air Force blue sky. The river, too, had turned a matching blue and the wind had stilled itself. I stood atop a dune and looked to the west at a golden cloudscape, mares' tails pointed like racing greyhounds running to the north, the sun's disc not quite visible behind low hill and cloud. I read my map in the ample light, reluctant to go to bed, then simply sat on the dune and blended with the universe for a while, delighting in the indescribable joy of merely being.

It is at such times of magnificent gentleness that one contemplates cosmology; the whys and the wherefores of existence. It is then that the great enigma of creation itself demands answers to unclear questions. I toyed with the popular Judaic concept of creation, and the Christian attempt of the Trinity to explain the nature and advent of the deity by making Him His own Son. But, I reflected, there were other concepts, no less valid, with their roots equally firm in antiquity and with, perhaps, a finer pedigree . . .

'How . . .?' asked the boy . . . and 'Why . . .? When . . .? Where . . .? And who?'

The man whose name, perhaps, was Olaf, settled the boy's

head on his breast and arranged his mind to tell of what was, and what had been.

'In the beginning,' he said, and his voice was hushed, 'when there was nothing, neither land, nor sea, not even a cloud for there was no sky in which to fly, there became a greaty empty gap in the nothingness. It was longer than could be thought . . . and wider than could be measured . . . and its depth went on forever . . . And the name of the gap was Ginnunga-gap.

'It was in Ginnunga-gap that all things began, and there time itself was born so that there could be a yesterday, a today, and a tomorrow. In all of time there was twilight, and in the twilight was All-father who holds sway over all things, no matter how small, and no matter how great. And what is the will of All-father comes into being.

'The first that All-father willed was that to the north would be a place of darkness, and of ice; and because He willed it, it was so. And this place He called Nifelheim, the home of mists.

'The second that All-father willed was that to the south would be a place of light, and of warmth; and because He willed it, it was so. And this He called Muspelheim, the home of brightness.

'Then it was that from the terrible cold of Nifelheim surged venomous streams of ice full of horror and evil. The streams ran south, and great icebergs rolled and crashed together above Ginnunga-gap as they sped towards Muspelheim.

'Then it was that from Muspelheim sprang mighty rays of heat full of beauty and goodness. The rays shone north above Ginnunga-gap and fell upon the rivers of ice, and calmed the cold anger with their warmth.

'Drops of water began to fall from the ice and they gathered together into an ocean. All-father willed; and because He had willed it the waters of the ocean became clay, and the clay became a mighty giant, the untamed power of nature.

'He was a mighty giant, and he had a mighty hunger.

All-father willed: and because He had willed it, more water became clay, and the clay became a giant cow from which flowed great rivers of milk which nourished the giant and caused him to fall into a deep sleep. And as he slept All-father took the sweat of his left armpit and from it He fashioned a woman, and the name of the woman was Bestla.

'But for the cow, the great nourisher, there was no grazing so she licked the salt from the ice-rock. On the third day that she licked there sprang from the rock a youth of great beauty in body and in mind. He was the first of the gods, and his name was Buri. Many were the gods who followed the divine Buri and shone in majesty from their home in Asgard.

'The son of Buri was Bör, and he fell in love with Bestla the daughter of the clay giant. Three sons she bore; Hönir the god of water and of the will, and Loki the god of fire and of evil; but her first-born was Oðin, the king of the gods. Oðin, the god of battles who brings the storm and wields the lightning for a sword; whose handmaidens, the Valkyries, consecrate heroes with the kiss of death and bear them away to Asgard, the home of the gods. First they are taken to Hell where the gods pass judgement and reject the unworthy, then on to Valhalla, the hall of the valiant, there to feast forever in the presence of mighty Oðin himself, in whom dwells the essence of all that is and could ever be; for He is All-father Oðin – the creator of creation, and of Himself.'

So ended the tale spoken by the man whose name, perhaps, was Olaf. He looked down at the head of the boy, sleeping at his breast, and wondered at the things he had said. Was it all a reality? He did not know . . . He did not know if the gods were real, or wise stories to explain that which was difficult of understanding. But of Oðin he was sure. There had to be an Oðin. Even the Christians, who worshipped dead men, even they had a living Oðin. Yes . . . there had to be an Oðin . . . or there would be nothing . . . nothing at all . . .

*   *   *

During the night the sky shed a little rain. The early morning was cloudy but occasionally a patch of blue would allow the sun to shine upon the black damp sand making the air humid. I ate a hot meal and began to walk south following the riverside. Before me, shadowy through distant curtains of rain, was Herðubreið thrusting from the plain thirty miles away. The world was a world of blacks, whites and greys. My feet crunched on the dead expanse of broken black lava, little geometric stones sharp to the touch. Here and there were great slabs of solidified lava, the ridges caused at the transition from liquid to solid now preserved and as permanent as anything can be on this island of geoviolence. This was a moonscape with a volcanic horizon all around. The Apollo astronauts trained here a little, this being the nearest to lunar conditions that their home planet could offer. It passed whimsically through my mind that if this was what they knew they would find then why did they bother going. Of course I knew that they had to go for the same reasons that I had come to Iceland, for when mankind ceases to go beyond the next frontier, be it in the physical, intellectual or spiritual universe, then the species will have commenced to die.

I wished to go twenty miles south before that night. There I would plan the assault on the world's biggest lava desert. There was, according to the map, a track of sorts running roughly in that direction which I would no doubt encounter at some stage, but for now I had had enough of tracks. There is a primitive excitement about making one's own way, ploughing one's own furrow despite the difficulties, that can never be eclipsed by the ease of passage on well-tried routes. There was the joy of accomplishment in the day and I began to sing; first in my mind, then to myself, and finally to the world's absent population, to tell them of my happiness. The bum notes drifted cacophonously over the plain as I sang old music-hall numbers, forgetting the words and filling in with anything that came to mind as I packed up my troubles in my old kit-bag and smiled – smiled – smiled all the long – long way to Tipperary.

By mid-morning the wind had changed direction and was blowing coldly from the north, bowling me gently south. I stopped to rest, sitting on a lava rock, and looked to the north. The sun had broken through the cloud in that direction and had heated the ground to the extent that a great heat-haze mirage-lake stretched, mirror-like, over acre upon acre, dotted with islets of lava. On the horizon volcanoes floated upon this enormous non-existent inland sea and were perfectly reflected in its surface. I had seen many such mirages in the hot deserts, but was pleasantly surprised to see one so close to the Arctic Circle.

To the south and the west, however, there was an entirely different picture. Thick black clouds hovered heavy with water which was falling in long streaks to the desert below. Herðubreið and the mountains beyond the lava desert had completely vanished and, despite the wind at ground level coming from the north, the entire storm was heading straight for me carried by southerly winds at about three thousand feet. I heaved my rucksack onto my back and went to meet it.

Soon I found myself on the track, which could hardly be glorified by that description as it consisted of an occasional wooden stake and a few Land Rover tracks meandering in varying degrees of proximity. The rain and lack of visibility were closing in so I decided to stick to the track for a while, my compasses having proved to be erratic once more. This, I had learned by diligent enquiry, was due to the magnetised volcanic rock. In the southern distance two dots appeared, shimmered a little, and gradually zoomed larger. As we converged they became two young men, woolly-hatted and winter-clad with enormous burdens upon their backs. Things were loosely tied to, and hanging from, their rucksacks which were loosely hanging from the young men. Pans and kettles clattered together and a sleeping-bag hung from string at a crazy angle. Tied, again, loosely over each rucksack was a sheet of black plastic which billowed behind like a square Viking sail as they battled north against the wind, teeth bared and lips thin on woebegone visages. Their whole appearance was that of being completely out of their element, like fish trying to swim in air; two once-bold men who had *fancied a go* and purchased the contents of a catalogue. They were not enjoying their holiday one little bit.

'Good morning,' they said in heavily Germanic English, forcing ritual smiles. I replied in like manner.

'How far is it to the road?' they wished to know.

'About twelve kilometres,' I told them. 'The ground is good. You should be there in three hours.' Their faces became vertically wrinkled. Obviously they had overestimated their velocity.

'How far is the river?' one of them asked.

'Half a kilometre.' I pointed to my left.

'Is it this side of the hill or the other side?'

I looked at the hill in question, fully six times the river's distance, and despaired for their future as outdoor men.

'This side,' I said, and with a weariness born of non-understanding they lurched towards the water, plastic sails billowing mightily behind as they clattered, tinker-like, upon their incompetent way. The wild places of the Earth are oft traversed by such. Some learn by experience to do things right and become learned in outdoor ways; most blunder through several trips and decide that bed and breakfast is both more comfortable, and in the long run cheaper, than doing it the hard way; still others stick their necks out just that bit too far, perhaps with inadequate equipment, a lack of basic knowledge, or without the exercise of proper caution. These latter are often gathered in, or narrowly missed by, Old Baldie and are the subjects of vast public indignation. It always seems to me, despite their incompetence, their lack of preparation and their downright omnipresent foolhardiness, that their sheer guts and determination set them head and shoulders above the clucking hens sitting fat, dumb and happy in their semi-detached batteries. Occasionally I have played a part in mountain rescue, usually as a rescuer but once as a rescuee, and never once have I heard a word of complaint either spoken or implied by those engaged upon it. We'll look after our own, and gladly.

I carried on with the wind becoming stronger at my back. Sometimes I would see one of the marker posts lying prone upon the ground like a fainted soldier who had given up trooping his colour. These I would resurrect and hammer into the ground with a lump of lava as a sort of modern version of placing a stone atop a cairn to placate the local gods.

These gods were not to be taken lightly, and certainly not in this particular venue of nature's latent anger. Thirty miles to the south, ahead and to the right of the birthday-cake of Herðubreið, arose the jagged horizon which was the Dyngjufjöll mountains dominated by the very active volcano of Askja. Its latest eruption, a minor one, had been in 1961, but the last great anger began to manifest in February of 1874 when extremely dense clouds of steam were observed from throughout eastern Iceland as the fissure upon which it stands, which stretches from Vatnajökull's ice-cap to fifty miles north beyond Dettifoss, began to widen like a latter-day Ginnungagap. All that December great earthquakes shook the north and on New Year's Day 1875 smoke billowed with the steam. On the second January day the earth quaked often, and on the third fire belched forth.

On February 18th the earth split along the fissure ten miles to my right as I walked south, at a place called Sveinagja, and vomited lava for several months. About this time four farmers from the north very bravely visited Askja and reported boiling mud and steam flowing from the crater.

On March 29th at three-thirty in the morning, tephra, which is consolidated volcanic ash, fell as far as forty-five miles to the east for an hour, then subsided and the air cleared a little. Later that morning the main eruption commenced. The air was filled with light-brown pumace in ever larger sizes of grain together with globules of red-hot glass and basaltic sand. Hell visited Earth until noon in the distant populated districts, but retreated later towards the crater where it rained down until noon on the following day.

The next year the crater was visited. Its interior had collapsed, probably into a lava chamber, forming a hollow known as a *caldera* about three miles west to east and one and a half miles north to south, which later filled partially to form a lake named Öskjuvatn. Someone calculated that a cubic mile or so of material was spewed out on this occasion, one of the greatest eruptions in Iceland's recorded history.

No, this was no place to fall foul of gods. I hammered in another marker post.

Evening brought the rain once more, unhappy cats and dogs falling all around and rushing in rapid rows along rivulets. I arrived at the spot where I wished to be, the swollen river churning powerfully past, fully a quarter of a mile wide. Of it I drank deeply for I had run out of water at midday. It was cool and refreshing as it trickled through my plumbing making my nasal passages pleasantly numb. The rain made transient circles on the water's surface and ran in streams from the hem and cuffs of my cagoul.

On the hillside I suddenly saw a small stone structure with a wooden door. I went to investigate. It was an emergency hut, unmarked on my map, with a corrugated tin roof and the door held closed with string to keep out animals. I untied the string and entered. It was a single room about eight feet square and five feet high with an earthen floor and nails in the roof beams to hang things from. The floor was dry and clean, and in a corner were a few dry sticks left courteously by the previous tenant. It was a mansion of a house, and it was to be mine for the night.

An hour later I was installed in my new home. Waterproofs were hanging from nails, my sleeping-bag was laid on my karrimat and a pile of wet wood stood drying in a corner. The rain had ceased and I sat by my front door tending my fire. Soon I was eating a hot meal and sipping steaming tea, looking out over the night-shining river, orange and blue like the sky above. It was as pleasant an end to a hard day as one could wish and when the last embers had winked out I lay down, content with my lot.

There is in Germany, adjacent to the fair town of Detmold, an enormous statue of an ancient winged-helmeted warrior. This is the Hermannsdenkmal, a memorial to one Hermann, a long-dead hero doubtless responsible for many brave deeds. Hermann, his metal structure green with age and peppered with RAF bullet holes, gazes out over the countryside from atop his fir-clad hill. Hermann the German is big. Hermann the German is solid. Hermann the German is immovable. In 1960, as a bulwark between Western Europe and the Russian hordes, I was stationed briefly beneath Hermann's fixed Teutonic stare. When I left the town I never thought to see that mighty man of action again; but I did!

It had been mid-morning when the sky-torrents had ceased to batter the tin roof of my dwelling. I had decided to spend another night there and to busy myself with the washing of clothes, the cleaning and resting of body and the taking of stock. The sun shone as I gathered sticks for my fire and Herðubreið towered a mere fifteen miles away. A speck moved along the track below the mountain. It became bigger, and bigger, and bigger. After a while the speck acquired legs and arms, and a head above solid shoulders. The giant, for giant he was, strode towards me, slow of gait but eating up the miles. In my mind, unbidden, came the words '*Fee! Fie! Fo! Fum!*' in time with his tread. He stopped in front of me and smelled the blood of an Englishman.

Well over six feet above seven-league boots his mouth split into a wide grin. His eyes, at a slightly higher altitude, were gentle and friendly eyes and his body was mighty as an oak. He spoke.

'Gut mornink!'

The rich deep bass reverberated from the hills and caused avalanches high on Herðubreið.

'Good morning,' I confirmed, my inadequate tenor sounding positively falsetto by comparison.

'Ach! Joo are Eenglisch?' he asked. Fissures appeared in the land and long-dead volcanoes were reactivated.

'Yes. And what is your country?' I enquired, knowing full well the answer.

'I am German,' he said, causing the people of Egilsstaðir to glance apprehensively at the sky. Indeed had he said that he was of any other nationality I could not have believed him. He never gave me his name but he was so obviously the reincarnated Hermann that it would have been blasphemous to suggest otherwise. Rejecting, reluctantly, fanciful thoughts of clay-giant connections, I asked him politely about the weight of his pack, which he said was roughly as heavy as my own but on Hermann it looked like a school satchel. We exchanged brief recent histories and immediate plans. He was walking and hitching throughout the island and was now bound for Lake Mývatn, a volcanic lake to the north. I mentioned my plan to cross the lava desert and a look of genuine pain crossed his face.

'Zere vill be new lava. It iss ferry difficult. I haff been on new lava. It vill cut up joor boots.' He pointed to his seven-league boots as an unexplained storm lashed the eastern seaboard of Greenland. The boots were deeply scarred throughout, both on soles and uppers. They had been good boots but were now sad and decrepit, though they were not old boots for there was yet a newness about the ankles. That they were boots on their last journey there could be little doubt.

'On ze new lava I make only von kilometre in von hour. Sometimes not so much. It iss ferry dangerous,' he warned as seismologists on North Sea oil rigs missed lunch. One kilometre per hour meant roughly half a mile an hour. The desert was about forty miles wide. If it was all new lava then there would be eighty hours of walking before reaching the river beyond. What new lava looked like I had no idea, but I was gratified that Hermann had experienced it and lived. If he could do it then so could I. Within me, like a waking serpent, stirred the fear of the unknown.

After the lava would come Sprengisandur, the black sand desert of the interior. I asked Hermann if he knew of it. He said that this was the area of the island's strongest winds, highest rainfall and lowest clouds, and that this was the worst time of the year. What did he know of the Hofsjökull glacier, I wished to know. He spoke of two experienced climbers whom he had recently met after they had retreated from the mighty Vatnajökull because of unsafe snow bridges over crevasses. Gloom and doom loomed large ahead.

Hermann's pack began to ring. It was a steady ring, an insistent ring which would brook no indifference. Hermann looked sadly resigned and with effortless ease swung his leaden pack from his shoulders to the ground. Lifting the top flap he plunged his arm into the depths and searched around blindly like an army cook whose false teeth have fallen into the stew. For some time he groped and finally, with a cry of triumph worthy of a cathedral pipe-organ, he withdrew a hand clutching a small electric alarm-clock. Theatrically he flicked a switch and the world was quiet once more save for the rumble of the river. He repacked his time-piece then, without visible effort, picked up his heavy burden with one hand and slung it onto his back.

'Zo!' he said with finality and a grin, 'I vill go nort. Gut luck mit der new lava!' A spade-like appendage of flesh, bone and sinew wrapped itself deftly around my hand and shook it gently. Then with a smile and a wave Hermann the German loped north whilst dedicated professors throughout Scandinavia diligently revised long-held theories of geomorphology.

For the rest of the day I pottered. Several road-posts were hammered erect and one or two large rocks were heaved out of the roadway to prevent their contact with exhaust systems. The main river was about half a mile away over mud-flats beyond the small rivulet close by. Deciding to encounter it I leaped from stone to stone over to the flats and strolled towards its banks. There were eider ducks on the river which kept their distance. I reached the bank and happily skimmed flat pebbles over its choppy surface as I had when a boy. Many years previously I had been introduced to solid and staid adulthood, but it hadn't taken. To this day I see adults as people set in their ways with no sense of adventure or wonder, and little inclined just to have fun. For many the searching innocence of youth returns upon retirement, but for most it is sadly lost forever when they tell themselves that they are grown-ups. 'Poor sods,' I thought as I skimmed another pebble and watched it go pat-pat-plop.

Suddenly my left leg vanished to the calf in quicksand. I threw myself backwards, lay on the solid ground and slowly eased the leg from the gripping clinging stuff. There is no danger in quicksand if one treats it as thick water. Contrary to popular belief it does not have the power to suck its hapless prisoner under. If one lies down in it then one will float and be able slowly to swim out. If one remains standing as fallible instinct dictates, then, as with water, down one will go. My body was on good solid sand and it was the work of half a minute or so to free my leg. Unfortunately my left knee is not a well knee which from time to time, of its own volition, decides to give me gyp. During the extraction process I had given it a fair old wrench and it began to protest like mad. This boded ill for the next day's rigours.

But such problems were all part of the game. By the time I had built my fire to cook my evening meal all apprehensions had departed. A fire can do that. It is much more than a functional thing: its therapeutic value is inestimable. A fire must be tended and kept alive, blown at occasionally and fed, and in return it will give of its life to its creator. I can fully understand why fire was worshipped. I ate, and drank tea, as the moon popped up above the hills, and in self-indulgent mood I put on another pan of water for a second cup. Then I just sat and enjoyed the fire, adding wood for a while and listening to its crackle. As the embers glowed their last I reflected that a fire had much in common with a dog in that it gave warmth and companionship. In fact it was better than a dog since it did not require to be led to someone else's doorstep in order to facilitate the movement of its bowels.

4   The Lava Desert

I had cornflakes for breakfast; big black cornflakes taller than a man. It was late morning when I saw them, stretching far out into the distance. I sat on top of a thirty-foot lava cliff, surveyed the problem, and worried.

That morning I had leaped from my house into a clear blue day. Old Baldie and I, like the gladiators of old, had prepared ourselves meticulously for the duel ahead. A final act of symbolism was to strap on My Father's Sword, an antler-handled sheath knife left to me by my father which came with me on every trip. It pleased me to believe in its power to ward off my enemy and, like my Viking ancestors, I held the primeval thought that I must die with sword in hand if I would enter Valhalla in Asgard and feast forever with Oðin.

I had hydrated myself to the point of saturation so that I had to walk carefully with head back to prevent spillage. My compasses had again proved erratic so navigation was to be by sight and sound, as on the moor. Twenty miles to the west, beyond the stratified lava, was the mountain massive of Bláfjall. Over 3,500 feet and sparsely capped with snow, it brooded low on the horizon. Here would be my next water, a meltwater stream which, according to the map, trickled from the summit onto the desert below. Over years of desert travel I had learned to mistrust indications of water on maps, or *paper water* as I called it. It was better to assume, if the source appeared to be small, that the next watering-place was dry and act accordingly. However it seemed a safe bet that there would be water beneath Bláfjall, and if there wasn't then there was certainly water in a large river, the Skjálfandafljót, some fifteen miles beyond.

Leaving my little house behind I turned my back on the wide river, my companion for four days, and set out for the lava with Herðubreið towering to my left. It was good to be on the move again. Here was the morning of the seventh day and I was a mere seven miles from the point I had reached on day three thanks to a two-day detour to the bridge and my day of rest. Now I was moving west again and I was happy about it, as if I were somehow paying a debt of honour.

The ground was much the same as on the river bank, sand and gravel dotted with black cow-pats of lava, so progress was quite swift. In under a couple of hours I had covered five miles and was happy with the world. Then I found myself standing atop the thirty-foot cliff looking at the cornflakes. Old Baldie grinned.

Lava comes in two visual types described by geologists, for some reason in the Hawaiian language, as *aa* (pronounced ah-ah), and *pahoehoe*. Both are chemically the same but whilst the surface of *pahoehoe* tends to be flat with some rope-like formations where the plastic surface-skin has wrinkled before solidifying, the surface of *aa* lava is broken and thrust upwards in jagged blocks of lava from truck-size to handy pocket-size by exploding gas-blisters beneath the surface. These cornflakes had originally been flat *pahoehoe* lava but when the surface had solidified the flow-rate of the lava must have changed, breaking up the surface and piling the slabs atop each other in a completely disorganised, patternless mass. *Aa* translates as 'a surface upon which one cannot walk barefoot', whilst *pahoehoe* means 'a surface upon which one *can* walk barefoot'. This latter says much for the quality of Hawaiian feet. As the whole field had cooled and contracted, great fissures appeared across my direction of travel and whole sections, miles wide, dropped to form rift valleys. It was from the edge of such a fissure cliff, formed during the great 1875 eruption, that I surveyed the scene of utter chaos. I was now on the edge of the mighty Askja fissure and seven miles ahead was Sveinagja from where all this lava had oozed a century previously, which, in geological time, was only yesterday.

For a while I sat and just stared. I had, during a lifetime of travel in remote places, encountered some pretty rough territory, but I had never seen anything that looked as rough as this. There did not seem to be a definite ground-level so progress would be slow. I filmed and photographed a little to remind me of my first encounter with the problem, then saddled up and gingerly picked my way down the brittle cliff-face by the easiest route I could find. All the rocks were sharp-edged and loose, and despite my care there were several slips. I reached the cornflakes and inspected them. They seemed to be of black basalt, thin, sharp-edged and brittle, and every one was loosely balanced upon others. The slabs were all at crazy angles and some must have weighed half a ton. Carefully I stepped onto a roughly horizontal flake some seven feet across. With a scrape and a crunch and a rumble it pivoted towards me and thudded hollowly to a new position. Holding my arms out instinctively for balance I moved forward. The slab crunched back to its former position and came to rest as a smaller but yet heavy flake fell over onto the spot I had just vacated, and with a loud crack broke into several pieces. Onto another flake I leaped, which slid sideways. I grabbed at another slab for balance and a lump came off in my hand. Clawing the air I regained my equilibrium only to lose it again when the moving slab beneath me jolted to a halt at an entirely new angle. 'This is bloody dangerous!' I commented in admiration to my bone-headed antagonist. Normally crossing broken country is much like ballet-dancing inasmuch as one balances upon a series of more or less solid points, tripping precisely from one to the next in as delicate a manner as mountain boots will allow. Progress here had much more in common with juggling. There were tentative thoughts of retreat, tinged with a little healthy fear of a lone accident, but my innate pigheadedness won the day. Carefully, very carefully, I stepped upon the next plate of lava.

Soon I got the hang of it. The idea was to keep the knees bent and anticipate movement in any direction. I estimated that I was moving at about one mile per hour. If this was the new lava that Hermann the German had spoken of, over which he had made only half that speed, things were not too bad at all.

Then I came upon the first fissure, a great crack in the ground about five feet or so wide and seemingly bottomless. I could see down its sheer sides for a hundred feet or so. Beyond this it continued downwards, Hell-black and terrifyingly unseen. It was at a right-angle to my direction of travel and seemed to stretch forever to the north and south. I knew that I could leap five feet quite comfortably, even with the weight of my pack to hold me back, but this knowledge had little importance when confronted with that great gaping chasm down which waited my lipless adversary. Imagination is infinitely stronger than knowledge or will-power. I headed south looking for a narrower place. A three-foot gap presented itself and, heart pounding with fear, I charged at the problem, flew the barrier, and landed gratefully on the other side. During the next hour there were two others to leap, each one holding less terrors than the last as familiarity bred contempt.

I was halted by a fifty-foot cliff, sharp-edged and clean to the cornflakes below. I thought that I might have to lower my rucksack down the cliff-face using the thin length of rope I carried for just such an eventuality, but decided to go south for a while to see what turned up. I found a place, very precarious and loose, and eventually slid and stumbled onto the lava plates with palms sweaty and breath heavy. The wind had risen to considerable strength, naturally in the opposite direction to me.

By mid-afternoon I had been up and down several of the

fifty-foot cliffs and was about ten miles from my hut by the river. Both my hands were bleeding front and back from cuts and scrapes caused by the sharp abrasive lava. My boots were deeply scarred and I was utterly exhausted, but there could be no question of calling it a day. Bláfjall and my next water were still ten miles away and I had to get much closer before I could bed down with anything approximating to peace of mind.

At four o'clock I allowed myself my first drink since leaving the river. I was pleased to see that very little water had leaked from the bottle. Just a small mouthful I took, though I really wanted much more. The next day, I knew, I would be in far greater need of it.

I had now reached Sveinagja, the source of all my ills. There was no obvious emission point of the century-old lava, the perpetual cornflakes covering the floor of a mile-wide rift valley bordered ahead by another fifty-foot cliff, the last, according to my map, towering intimidatingly above and, like the great wall of China, seemingly going on forever. I searched for a breach in the fortress and, finding what looked like a possible route, commenced the climb. That climb would have been difficult even had I not suffered from vertigo. Fear of heights had assailed me most of my life. I had taken up tree-climbing as a child and rock-climbing as a youth, in order to convince myself and others that I had no fear of high places. And indeed, because I had beaten the fear and accomplished these things, the fear had left me, but only whilst these things continued to be practised. Twenty years previously a climbing accident had put me out of action for a number of years due to a smashed vertebra. I had never returned to serious rock work for in the interim climbing had become a sport. I hated sport. As a result acute vertigo had returned to the extent that it was a worrying thing to stand upon a chair to change a light-bulb.

With a care born of my fears I slowly ascended that basalt wall, testing each hand- and foot-hold and recalling past skills. The ground became more remote and hands and legs ached with the exertion of it as inch by inch I conquered the mighty bastion. It seemed an age later when I dragged myself and my pack over the rim and onto the flat top. I lay panting for a few minutes, gazing out over the broken lava I had lately traversed. Then I stood in justifiable triumph to see a great fissure, over ten feet wide, betwixt me and the plateau. I had just spent a great deal of time and mental and physical energy climbing a flake ten feet away from the cliff itself and the only way forward was to go back down again. I was less than pleased; quite a bit less!

When I eventually gained the plateau I noticed a definite up-slope of the land, not steep but consistent and therefore specifically designed to steadily sap any remaining energy. *Onward* was the cry as I ordered my reluctant body to continue the assault. The sun, brilliant and low on the horizon ahead, shone blindingly into my eyes as another fissure appeared, a mere three or four feet across. I had jumped about ten of these of late and was becoming quite blasé about the whole thing. Breaking into a shambling trot I neared the edge and thrust my left foot down hard to commence my leap. Old Baldie struck!

My foot shot from under me and I found myself in mid-air, slowly turning over onto my back. Everything was happening incredibly slowly as my mind, aware of my extreme danger, switched onto a lower rate of perception allowing for quicker reaction. I caught a glimpse of the yawning depths and imagined myself bouncing and scraping down-down-down. My rucksack hit the edge of the chasm on the take-off side and I grabbed wildly with my right hand for something to hold onto as I felt myself teeter towards the abyss. My hand found a hold and my arm pulled-pulled-pulled me away from the edge. An inch or two – just an inch or two would do to redress the balance in favour of solid ground. The hold held and I froze.

Incongruously an entirely separate part of my mind said, quite calmly, 'Switch on your tape-recorder and record this.

It's important!' The machine was in my right breast pocket and my left hand was close to it so I did so. '*Shit!*' I said to it. Every move I made from then on I described on tape in a very worried voice indeed.

Quickly I took stock of the situation. I was lying on my rucksack, attached to it by shoulder and waist straps. My right buttock and leg were on the lip of the crack but my left buttock and leg were in air. Everything beneath me was loose. My heart pounded like a bass drum and I realised that I had ceased to breathe. Gently I released the pent-up air in my lungs; very slowly I sucked in more oxygen as I thought out my next move.

My balance was still in favour of the chasm so I needed to roll away from it to my right. To do this I had to unstrap the heavy rucksack, which from that angle was immovable. Slowly I brought my left hand over to the waist strap quick-release buckle and unsnapped it. The buckle flew sideways and the slight movement dislodged a rock which fell, hitting the sides for an age until the hitting was too remote to hear. I noticed that my mouth was dry, and somehow this seemed very important.

Next I had to remove my left shoulder strap. It was tight and firm against my shoulder. Clearly it would have to be slackened. My right hand, my only anchor, was beginning to tire as my left fumbled with the adjustment buckle. The strap went slack. Deliberately, and with much grunting, I eased my hand through the strap loop and slid it over my shoulder until I was free of it, explaining my movements to my tape-recorder in a hesitant voice.

Then, degree by degree, I turned to my right, pulling and gripping with my right hand. Suddenly it was done. I was kneeling on solid ground. My rucksack, its right strap still around my arm, slid towards the drop but it was no problem to drag it back. Great gulps of air surged into my starved lungs as I babbled my relief into my tape-recorder.

Icebergs calving into Jökulsárlón at one of the snouts of Vatnajökull, 'the biggest glacier in Europe'. The lake runs into the sea along the world's shortest river, fully half a mile long

The beginning: the fjord of Seyðisfjörður and the Arctic Ocean. Beyond, six hundred miles distant, the Viking mainland

Möðrudalur; all of it. A house, a church, a café and a small, camera-shy ginger dog

The approach to the lava desert, a moonscape with a volcanic horizon all round. The Apollo astronauts trained here

Lunch-time at the emergency hut where I rested before tackling the world's biggest lava desert

Herðubreið, the birthday-cake mountain which dominated my horizon for days, as seen from the emergency hut

A fissure similar to the one down which Old Baldie almost threw me to my death

Cornflakes for breakfast. I had never seen terrain as rough as this lava desert. Bláfjall, my next possibility of water, is seventeen miles away on the horizon

Black volcanic sand drifts into dunes as trackless as the Sahara. A broken ankle here would almost certainly be a sentence of death

Lake Öskjuvatn in the crater of Askja, blasted during the eruption of 1875 when the lava desert was formed. The crater Viti is in the foreground

Looking down the Tungnafellsjökull valley. The inaccessible Hofsjökull, like the upturned dinner-plate of Oðin, is beyond

The summit and glacier of Tungnafellsjökull. Four-thirty p.m., darkness approaching and the weather closing in. Decision time!

Looking back over the defeated glacier. Five-thirty p.m., clouds dropping rapidly but the summit still beckoning a half-hour away. No contest!

Gullfoss, the golden waterfall, photographed from the tourist side. Old Baldie hung around the extreme right of the upper fall

Strokkur, the mini-geysir. The king is dead . . . Long live the king. Whereas the Great Geysir has to have soap powder poured into it to induce occasional activity, Strokkur erupts vigorously every ten minutes

Reykjavik. Journey's end with the Denmark Strait beyond and not a dog in sight

'Shit! . . . That bugger's deep! . . . Right. I've rolled away from the edge . . . Bloody Hell . . . I'm getting careless. I'm over-tired and I'm getting careless. I didn't test that foot-hold . . . I must have a good rest. This is dangerous . . . God that was close . . . I'll have a rest . . .'

Old Baldie had made his move, and he had failed again. I lay on my back beside the fissure, chest heaving, water-bottle in my blood-streaked hand, staring up at the evening sky and grinning the stupidest of grins.

When I was rested I strapped on my load and leaped the chasm that had so nearly been my grave. Eyes squinting in the sun I continued west, now actively searching for somewhere to spend the night. A strange patch of territory stretched before me, light green and as far as the eye could see to left and right. I stopped at its edge. If the previous terrain was cornflakes then this was puffed wheat, each grain varying in size from tennis- to basket-ball. A blanket of lichen covered it all so that the points of contact were indistinct. I touched it with my boot and it crunched like coke. There was no visible way around so I would have to cross it. With thoughts of possible hidden fissures beneath I hesitantly embarked into the unknown. My first impression of coke continued as the loose lumps of cinder beneath the lichen shifted under my weight. Some were in steep-sided piles a man high, like Henry Moore sculptures long forgotten in a distant future time.

For twenty minutes or so I picked my stumbling way through this alien landscape, wary as a cat on snow, and eventually gained the other side. The cornflakes had gone, to be replaced by solid slabs of lava with black sand and gravel between. Here and there the sand had drifted into ridges, clean-edged and reminiscent of Africa's shifting sands. Progress was swifter now as I walked into the ever-lowering sun, the wind whipping up the sand and making my teeth uncomfortably gritty.

At about nine o'clock my legs stopped work for the day. 'Thus far and no further!' they told me, and there was no appeal.

Nearby was a sheltered hollow with ten-foot lava walls around and a sand and gravel floor. That was to be my home for the night. Soon my bivi was pitched and all made ship-shape. Surprisingly there was a little greenery clinging close to the soil and, here and there, a few twigs of dead wood for a small fire. There wasn't enough for a cooked meal, even had I sufficient water for such an indulgence, which I hadn't. There was, however, ample of each for a good strong brew to follow vacuum-packed salami and three-day-old bread, an excellent repast. There were then the usual rituals of recording recent events and changing films in cameras before I fell asleep half-way through a small bar of chocolate.

I slept solid and deep for ten hours. The previous night's chocolate was polished off, together with another bar and a few sips of water. To eat anything more was not a good idea as I was down to about half a pint of water with no prospects of any more until about midday at the earliest, and to eat is to invoke thirst. Dehydration was becoming apparent as my mouth dried. The little that I did drink I sloshed around my mouth, forcing it through teeth and washing fur from tongue before swallowing it down. By nine o'clock I was on my way again in the cold and windy morning. Soon I reached the top of the rise and could see, for the first time, the full height of Bláfjall, like a great beached whale six miles away. The snow on its summit ridge was sparse and I could just make out the gully down which the meltwaters would be flowing. The going was much easier as the land now sloped downwards. Herðubreið had become hidden behind hills to my left and my world was now dominated by the expanding Bláfjall and its meltwater promise.

I saw three sheep, warm in brilliant cream coats, wandering the desert. Sheep must drink regularly so either there was an oasis of water on this desert or they were three very thirsty sheep. Parched as I was I resisted the temptation to search for this speculative water and continued on towards the better bet.

Clouds were heavy and hovering just above Bláfjall as I continued over that cold, vast and barren land. I felt no stiffness of limbs in the morning now as the *baptism of fire* principle once more proved its worth, but I was very tired and weak. The previous day's exertions had taken their toll and my body wanted only to rest. My mind knew, however, that to rest was, quite simply, to die. I was almost out of water and without water the human body ceases to function. I could not allow my body to dictate terms; however, it had a point. I compromised by walking for forty-five minutes and resting for fifteen minutes, and was absolutely meticulous in the timing.

The summit of Bláfjall vanished and the thick cloud began to creep inexorably down its flanks as the cloud ceiling lowered above me. This was worrying because as I approached Bláfjall I expected the mountain to shelter me from the constant wind, and to change the direction of whatever wind remained. Since my compasses were unreliable, if vision was blotted out and wind was no longer constant then I would have severe navigational problems. I permitted myself to worry a little and quickened my pace to lower my altitude.

Sand became more and more the dominant feature of the land as the morning wore on. There were great knolls of lava some twenty feet high which had been thrust up when semi-molten by the boiling lava beneath, but between these was drifting sand piled in dunes, or like giant snow-drifts against ridges of basalt.

Happily the cloud began to rise and eventually the mountain tops became visible again. The land suddenly sloped rapidly away and I could see the whole extent of the ground between Bláfjall and me. For a mile or so it was a sandy plain, and then more broken lava cornflakes. From the summit

snows an intermittent silver trickle dropped down towards
the desert, becoming fainter as it lost altitude and finally, at a
height of some five hundred feet above the plain, petered out,
soaked into the thirsty rock. I expressed my verbose dis-
approval in fluent Anglo-Saxon.

It was decision time. I had with me a mere mouthful of
water and thirst was beginning to rage. A further scrutiny of
the map showed a possibility of water four miles or so to the
north-west, at the base of Bláfjall to my right. A small thin line
of blue cut through a minute area of green on my map denoting a stream and an unlikely area of pasture. I looked in that
direction, over the miles of cornflakes, and saw nothing but
grey and black. Was it more *paper water*? I had no way of
knowing. The only way to find out was to go there. This meant
that subsequently I would have to go around the right-hand
side of the mountain and descend what looked like thousand-
foot cliffs to the plain below, not a pleasant prospect, followed
by twenty miles of very vague terrain to the Skjálfandafljót
river. The alternative, to the left of the mountain, looked
shorter and easier but with even less chance of water.

I decided to go for the pasture. There seemed little point in
carrying a mouthful of water so I drank it, slowly and with
relish. There was as yet no real mortal danger in my state of
dehydration, but I knew from experience that the next few
hours would not be comfortable and if there was indeed no
water at the pasture then I would begin to be in trouble.

A quick film and photo session was slipped into my rest
period and I was off again down the steep slope of soft sand
towards the first cornflakes. Soon I was repeating my balanc-
ing act and opening up new and old cuts in my hands. An
hour later thirst had become the most important thing in my
mind, much more important than fatigue or pain. My knee,
which I had wrenched in the quicksand, had been very painful
all day, and under normal circumstances that pain would have
been excruciating, but there was no place in my mind for pain;

there was room only for thirst. Sucking mints helped, but soon even that was no comfort as saliva became as thick as tar. Because of my heavy burden and physical exertions I was dehydrating at a much faster pace than I had ancitipated. My skin was wet and clammy, and cold in the risen wind.

During a rest period I saw in the distance, where the pasture should be, a brilliant white dot. It couldn't have been a natural phenomenon so it must have been man-made. I remembered mankind, and that I was a member of that species. It was an interesting thought. My whole being became focused upon that white dot. The reaching of that white dot was all that mattered in the world. To put out my hand and touch the works of men was a desperate need and to this end I moved over the lava. All would be well, thirst would go, pain would go, fatigue would go, if I could only reach that Holy Grail of a white dot at the bottom of the mountain.

The white dot became a white square, further evidence of its human manufacture. Walk as I might it would not come closer, always moving tantalisingly out of reach. The terrain was now solid outcrops of lava that had to be climbed over, hillock after hillock of solid cold stone, ridged and cracked and black. Then the white square gave up the chase and became a cubic hut amid a grassy meadow with dots of white sheep everywhere; and out of the mountainside, as if smitten by the mighty challenging rod of Moses, came forth water.

It was the merest trickle of water, cool and clear, running down a little cleft of damp sand flanked by light green spongy moss. I filled my cup carefully so that I did not disturb the sand, and drank the liquid of life. The finest of wines could not have tasted sweeter than that water trickling down the mountainside in the desert. Gratefully I drank my fill and filled my bottle. As predicted, thirst, pain and fatigue vanished in an instant to become a bitter half-memory. The world was a wonderful place and joy ranged unfettered.

The white hut was five minutes away so I went to investigate. It was the back of a van complete with two curtained windows and a locked door. Peering through the windows I saw two bench beds, a cupboard, and a carpeted floor, all fresh and neat. A name-plate on a post proclaimed 'Barð', a poetic name for an idyllic setting. And idyllic it certainly was. This was Shangri-La, a square mile of rich green meadow with clover, and purple and white flowers bobbing in a gentle breeze. The sun came out making the greens greener and the whites more brilliant. The sheep contentedly grazed, their wool clean and neatly arranged. If I were an upland sheep then this would be where I would wish to spend my days. Around and about, in all directions, lay the black and forbidding badlands, but here was a brief glimpse of Nirvana, of Eden, of that Never-Never Land of legend flowing with milk and honey.

Another stream, larger than the first, flowed past 'Barð'. I sat on its bank and ate sardines and ancient bread. It was mid-afternoon and I was ready for a good rest. After an hour or so, much recovered and possessed of new life, I departed from 'Barð' and set out north to skirt the mountain. A Land Rover track cut through the meadow and it seemed a good idea to follow it for a while. The sheep bade me farewell as I passed. Half an hour later the grass, the clover, the stream and the sheep came to an end. My dream was over and I was back to the hard reality of lava slabs and black gravel. Indeed I might well have taken it for a dream had it not been for the evidence of my water-bottle, full and heavy in its pocket.

The vehicle tracks meandered here and there to avoid the more difficult terrain so I played it by ear, sometimes following them and sometimes cutting across a great loop by a little scrambling. At about five o'clock I topped a rise and saw Lake Mývatn, Midge-lake, about six miles to the north-west. It covered almost my whole field of vision in that direction with islets dotting its surface and volcanoes at its far shore. Beyond, thirty miles away, the snow-capped coastal mountains hid the

Arctic sea and nothing but a small arm of Greenland barred the way to the North Pole itself.

The lake beckoned and I went. A short time later I found a great canyon gouged out of the lava by millions of spring torrents. It was delicate work to descend the loose red-tinged shale to the dry water-course below, and to follow the channel with its rocks worn into fantastic smooth sculptures by the power and doggedness of nature. For over a thousand feet I dropped carefully down towards the plain below and it was almost seven o'clock when I finally stepped from the mountain onto the plain. I was greeted by the flies.

There was no wind at the base of the mountain and the flies began to accumulate about my head. At first it was just a mild annoyance as the little black hump-backed flies wheened past ears and eyes. They neither bit nor stung and I wafted them away in a casual manner. They didn't go of course, but simply sent for their fellows who buzzed even closer and walked over spectacles. I stopped, dug out some insect repellent, and poured some onto my hand. Several flies landed on that hand, gathered around the pool of clear, oily liquid and began to drink. Several others dived into the aromatic centre of the pool and gleefully snuffed out their lives. This did not augur well for my future comfort.

I spread the stuff upon my face and hair and, contrary to instructions, managed to get some into my eyes and mouth. Inevitably a little went onto my spectacle frames and their plastic parts began to melt; but still the flies came, careening around in a holding pattern until squadron after squadron peeled off and made kamikazi swoops onto the headquarters of the invader. Thousands of dying flies adhered to the repellent on my face, around my spectacles and in my beard, wriggling out their lives for the glory of Iceland. And still they came, writhing and humming in my hair, crawling into stinging eyes and over stinging lips into stinging mouth. Fornication occurred in nasal passages and loud attempts were made at ingress to the middle ear. The sky was black with moving dots and vision was impaired by their sheer numbers. To wipe my face was to crush hundreds. The more repellent I applied, the more it stung my eyes and mouth, and the more the flies came. They were no longer an annoyance but a definite threat to life and limb. It was difficult to keep my nose free of them so that I could breathe. I blew it, and blew it again, caring not where the mixture of mucus and flies went. My mouth I kept tightly closed as the taste of crushed flies and repellent was horrific. I was again on broken lava and passage was incredibly slow and dangerous because of diminished sight. Fear and frustration manifested themselves, a sure combination to bring about madness. I began to sweat and the sweat carried more repellent into my eyes. My right eye closed in pain and would not open. Forward I stumbled, not sure in which direction I was headed but needing to keep going in the certain knowledge that somewhere out there was a place that was fly-free, and in the conviction that I would reach it if I kept moving. Emotions alternated. Sheer terror flashed from time to time and anger, black and self-righteously evil, roared through my soul. I wished vehemently for belief in the great god Oðin so that I could yell my hatred into his face. I tried to invent such a god to demand of him flood, or gale, or Vulcanic fire, or anything that would rid me of the flies, the flies, the flies.

Logical thought had become difficult as pure surging emotion ground me in its grip. I detested this island with its ugliness of deserts, its expensive necessities, its waterlessness and its flies. My strength ebbed as anger gave way to depression. I *had* to stop and rest so I sat on a lava slab, propping my rucksack on another slab to take the weight from my shoulders. From the positions of the surrounding hills I ascertained my approximate position on the map. It seemed that if I were to go towards a three-thousand-foot-plus mountain named Sellandafjall, in whose shadow I was, then I should leave the lava and reach a gravel plain. The lava had become even worse than anything previously encountered and, with the able assistance of the flies, was destroying my body and soul. It was about nine p.m. and I was low on water. About six miles away there was the possibility of water as, according to the map, a small stream ran across the gravel plain north to Lake Mývatn. I resolved to reach the stream before sleep that night.

Heaving up my rucksack I led my retinue towards the mountain, staggering and stumbling and cursing. The air was black with insects and blue with invective as once again my hands began to bleed. Insect repellent entered the cuts and stung like the stings of wasps. Perhaps an hour later I stood on the gravel plain and turned for the water. A Land Rover track appeared. It may have been the one which I had followed for a while from Shangri-La. In any case it was going roughly in my direction. I followed it. It saved me the trouble of thinking and deliberating. Just keep one track on each side and march mindlessly forward, eff – eye – eff – eye – eff – eye – eff!

As the sun sank lower, and the night advanced to semi-dark, a gentle breeze sprang up. It was wonderfully strong enough to blow away the flies. One or two hundred, more determined than the rest, stayed for a while, but soon they too were gone. I have never been so grateful for loneliness. The flies in my mouth I spat out, together with as much of the cloying, stinging, repellent as I could, and sloshed a little of my precious water around my teeth and tongue to rid myself of as much of the horrible stuff as possible. A small debate followed as to whether I should drink that water, now mixed with chemicals, or spit it out. My desert experiences led me to thoughts of conservation, but I finally decided not to risk the imbibing of even a small quantity of poison. Feeling a great sense of loss I spat the tablespoonful onto the gravel. With my handkerchief I wiped as much of the repellent from my face and eyelids as possible and found that, with pain, I could open my right eye for the first time in hours. With a shock my vision became three-dimensional again.

The tracks wandered amongst low slag hillocks, first left and then right. Unaware of any sense of direction I finally had to admit that I was lost. Doggedly I followed the track knowing that it must go somewhere, and no longer really caring where. At ten minutes to ten I gave up the struggle. Completely demoralised I simply flopped down onto the gravel, rucksack and all, and lay there panting gently, utterly spent in body, mind and soul. After a while I stirred myself sufficiently to erect my shelter and crawl inside like a wounded cur into his kennel, spreading out my cagoul to catch any rain that might fall in the night. Then I slept.

A sand-storm battered my bivi as I lurched into consciousness. The grains rattled onto the skin in violent gusts. It was cold and the world outside my haven was uninviting. Every limb, every muscle, every sinew ached. Chewing a bar of breakfast chocolate I perused my map. I knew my approximate position and estimated my next water to be about three hours away, if it existed. The chocolate was thick in my mouth and stuck my tongue to my palate. The previous night I had put my water-bottle, containing perhaps a wine-glass of water, outside and away from the tent to prevent myself from drinking it before morning when I knew I would need it most. But for boots and socks I was still fully clothed, having had neither the strength nor the inclination to undress the previous night. Depression was yet heavy upon me and to stay in that little cave of comparative comfort was an eminently desirable thing. But thirst won the day, as it always would, and I crawled into the grey, stinging world of wind and cold.

As I put on my socks and boots I noticed that my feet were red and swollen, like two little piggies bound for market, and when I stood they protested greatly. I drank half of my very cold water, beautiful nectar of life, and packed away everything. The night had brought no rain so my spread cagoul was bone-dry. There had been enough depression for one week, I decided, so forcing a face-cracking smile I sang the daftest songs I could think of and stomped my way along the Land Rover tracks. The thick clouds were almost low enough to touch and the air was damp with their proximity. Sometimes I followed the track and sometimes I cut off a corner. It took an age for the great cloud-clad bulk of the mountain to begin to move noticeably backwards. Periodically I rested, then on again through the greyness of slag and lava slabs, thinking of water trickling in streams, bouncing over boulders, falling over shelves and rushing down valleys. After two hours I drank the last of my little hoard of water and carried on-on-on towards the stream.

It was midday when I found it, a lazy tired trickle in a deeply gouged gully. Wondrous it was, and a giver of life. Happiness was no longer artificially imposed, but real and from the heart. I drank, washed my face and feet, washed flies from my beard and hair, became thoroughly wet and gloried in it. Half an hour later I left the stream and, with a full bottle and heart, strode westwards towards the river over ten miles away. There was no hurry now as I knew that there would be water there and I had an ample supply with me. Rests were happily frequent and long. The land had flattened to an easily traversed undulating plain of gravel and flat lava slabs. Soon after the stream the Land Rover tracks had veered north so I had left them in favour of a direct line to the river, keeping my course straight by reference to the distant western hills.

At four in the afternoon the plain suddenly dropped from me and there was the Skjálfandafljót, a quarter-mile wide, rolling northward along the valley. Beyond was the track for the mighty sand desert of Sprengisandur to the south-west, and to the north, an hour away, a massive suspension bridge to carry me there. The lava desert was behind me. The biggest lava desert in the world, and the worst terrain I had ever experienced, had been beaten. With that deep contentment that has nothing to do with comfort I loped in triumph towards the great curved finishing-post of the bridge.

5   The Sand

I oozed into wakefulness to the rustle of leaves. At sunset the previous night I had found a wood straddling the track about three hours south of the bridge. Dead wood in profusion meant a hot meal and contented, full-bellied sleep. Now the sleep was over and small birds chirruped, 'Get up! Get up! Get up!'

'Sod off! Sod off! Sod off!' I replied, but they insisted with the indisputable authority of Mother Frigga herself.

The Skjálfandafljót, turgid and swirling, was close by and I managed to obtain breakfast water which was almost transparent. Soon the shoulder-aching load was upon me again and I turned south into a rising wind topped by gathering storm-clouds. Before me was the prospect of sixty miles of I knew not what; my destination a hut in the middle of Sprengisandur, the great volcanic sand desert which covers the centre of Iceland. There I would decide my next move, whether to try for the Hofsjökull glacier or continue on through another sixty miles of desert. But that was for the future, a future about three days away, as remote and inevitable as Christmas seems in July. For now it was Sprengisandur, and tomorrow it would be Sprengisandur, and the next day it would, in all probability, be Sprengisandur.

Geologists describe Sprengisandur as a periglacial desert. This means that when the great ice-age glaciers covered the whole of this land their perpetual ponderous flowing had ground the underlying black volcanic basalt to sand, like the great Mill of God. When the ice retreated to the remaining glaciers it left behind, all over central Iceland, a black sandy plateau three thousand feet above the North Atlantic. The meltwaters of the remaining glaciers had gouged deep channels through the black wastelands along which they sped from spring thaw to autumn freeze.

I followed the vehicle tracks south, tracks that had grooved the earth to a depth that, in England, would almost have achieved the status of a farm track to some rarely visited field. This track I had resolved to follow for the present since it seemed the most practical route across that remote expanse. My trees thinned out and vanished, and with it my fuel. There were a few sticks strapped to my pack, sufficient for a single meal, but beyond that it would probably be cold meat and stale bread for sustenance. I passed a small cluster of still houses and went through a farm gate which blocked the track, then onward into a dead landscape of rolling black slag, monotonously curvy and flattening to a grey horizon.

The track went steeply up, then steeply down. Inclines fluctuated between about one in ten and one in four. Now and again a pair of tyre-marks would leave the main track and plough an independent furrow. Sometimes I would follow these, but always, like sad prodigals, we would return to the ways of the righteous majority. The wind became stronger, the sky darker and the air colder. Most of the slopes had been upward so that eventually the ground met the low storm-clouds and was devoured by them. I walked the grey ribbon road that came from swirling grey cloud thirty yards ahead, passed beneath my feet, and vanished back into grey cloud thirty yards behind. My world was a sixty-yard circle of vision, hazy at the edges, with only the track as a point of reference. Soon the yards became feet, and still the wind rose forcing the cloud's dankness into my body and swamping any hidden joys. I remembered Hermann the German's description of the Sprengisandur weather. The island's strongest winds, lowest clouds and highest rainfall, he had promised. Right on cue the rain sprang from the wings and vigorously made itself known.

Since I was within the cloud it was fine rain, its minute droplets mixed with the air to form what was simply a wet wind. My clothing kept me dry but, since the wind was coming from directly ahead, the thin spray covered my spectacles despite my normally protective wired hood. This caused the inside of the glass to mist over and effectively blotted out all vision in that miserable manifestation of frustration known only to the spectacle-wearer. Some semblance of vision was maintained by constantly rubbing the lenses with fingers, but mostly it was simply a case of following the vaguely different shade of grey which I knew to be the track.

The wind increased some more so that even down steep slopes, despite my heavy load, a great deal of traction had to be employed in order to make headway. The air was solid and to pass through it was like constantly pushing a heavy steel door, and it gusted so that one could never get complacent. Often it would almost throw me to the ground, but always I made a staggering recovery. My strength ebbed causing rests to become longer and more frequent. By midday I was walking for forty-five minutes and resting for fifteen. This was adaptable since if I found an outcrop of rock, or a hollow in the slag, anything that reduced the power of the wind, I would crawl into it for a short recovery time. During one of these halts I even strapped my bulky Karrimat and fuel sticks to the back of the rucksack along its vertical axis to cut down wind resistance. It seemed to have quite a beneficial effect.

The land levelled out, by which I mean that there were roughly as many uphill bits as there were downhill bits. The one blessing of my situation was the absence of flies, and from this thought I took great solace. The wind, slightly above freezing point, never let up; and it howled, and roared, and screamed like the sepulchral wailing of Hel, the Queen of the Dead. Suddenly a new sound broke into my consciousness, a strange unearthly sound, intermittent and insistent. I moved my hood from an ear to ascertain its direction. It was from behind. I wheeled around and there was Hel herself, Old Baldie in his Nordic manifestation, eyes shining through the swirling cloud and voice calling to the damned to receive my soul. I rubbed the condensation from my lenses and saw the headlights of the Land Rover whose passage I was blocking. The driver, seeing that I had observed him, stopped honking his horn. He was German and offered me a lift in the already crowded interior, but I reluctantly declined. He was obviously puzzled at this but, putting it down to the well-known masochism of the English, departed with a wave.

In all the time that I was in Iceland I never once mentioned to anyone the children's hospital charity aspect of my journey, the reason why I refused a number of lifts. I later analysed my feelings on the matter and concluded that far from reasons of self-conscious altruism, this was because I was secretly ashamed that such charities were necessary in my land, one of the richest countries on Earth, where it was deemed politically expedient to give the destruction of life so much greater priority than the preservation of its young.

In the mid-afternoon the cloud thinned and lifted. Visibility stretched to a hazy horizon. There was little to see. The rolling dunes of grey-black sand rolled on, and on, and on, cold, dank and featureless.

Sprengisandur – Sprengisandur.
Bloody great slag-heap, Sprengisandur!

There was only the track. Occasionally a pool of grey muddy water appeared, undrinkably opaque, its surface lashed by the constant wind. The rain had mostly left with the cloud so that at least the wind was dryish. The country was ugly, and monotonous, and incredibly uniform. For mile after mile after identical mile I went on, on, on. The sun was invisible and not even a glow showed its direction beyond the frantically rearranging clouds.

Something caught my eye alongside the track, perhaps a quarter of a mile away, and was gone. There was something there. I was sure that I had seen something very small and distinctly at odds with the landscape. I walked on, searching the land with minute scrutiny. There it was again, brilliant red and minute, like a glimpse of Mars on a clear night. I quickened my pace and homed in on it. Suddenly, there it was beneath my feet, wet and shining like a ruby on black velvet. I picked it up and read the inscription on its side.

'ZWANZIG ZIGARETTEN', announced the crumpled packet through the torn cellophane. I joyfully read the manufacturer's name and the location of the German factory wherein the absent cigarettes had been fashioned, then read them again, and again, happy as a child on Christmas morning, all thoughts of tediousness gone. I concluded that Iceland was the only country I had ever encountered that could be improved by litter.

The slopes of the track levelled out and the land became an even more monotonous plain with no protection whatsoever from the wind. It just didn't seem worth the effort to eat as this would break the routine of walk, rest, walk, rest, walk, rest, walk. My target for the day had been twenty miles, expecting to arrive at the hut at the desert's centre in three days. I passed the twenty-mile point and continued, aiming now for thirty miles since I was in reasonable condition and I had no wish to prolong my journey over Sprengisandur for one hour more than was absolutely necessary. There was no joy of battle in it, nor sense of achievement at the miles behind; just an automatic putting of one foot before the other in the knowledge that eventually would come journey's end. At the beginning of Sprengisandur I had taken one still photograph and a few feet of film, just as a matter of record. There seemed little point in using my cameras again. My tape-recorder, too, remained unused as there was nothing to say. It was that kind of day.

Sprengisandur – Sprengisandur.
Bloody great wind-tunnel – Sprengisandur!

Gradually the light faded, and with it the wind. At about eight all the factors of my existence suggested that I should halt for the night. My body had to be ordered to stop walking, like knocking a car out of gear and applying the brakes. It seemed momentarily strange to be static. There was a slightly sheltering hollow where I pitched my bivi, feet towards the wind, making sure that there were no vehicle tracks crossing the site. It could be unpleasant to wake beneath a Land Rover. Supper was salami with stale, and by now evil-smelling bread, washed down by half of my remaining pint of water and foreign bodies. There had been a damp stream bed a half-mile back, marked in blue on my map. More paper water. The morrow promised several possibilities, but for now there was the prospect of sleep. My feet were again swollen and, since they were no longer being punished, sensation began to return. Sharp needle pains shot through the soles like the return of circulation to cold-numbed hands. Legs began to stiffen, and shoulders. Soon sleep would be kept at bay no longer and I succumbed . . .

For ten solid and undisturbed hours I slept, I who was normally happy with little over six. By eight, with a belly partially appeased by something objectionable, I was on my way again. Nothing had changed about me. The wind had risen in opposition once more and the sky was still a translucent grey. Still the ground was damp black sand which rolled on to the circular horizon. Then I noticed that the horizon from the west to the south-west was lighter than the sky, a thin line of near-white for mile after mile. I checked the map and, sure enough, confirmed the sighting of Hofsjökull, the great circular glacier which was possibly my next challenge. Twenty miles away and twenty-five miles across, it was; twenty-five miles of moving ice and gaping crevass. *Glacier*, the word itself had a magic ring to it, like *Samarkand*, or *Atlantis*, or *Dragon*. Something fabulous one half-assumed to exist, but had never encountered. As if by the hand of mighty Oðin the clouds parted over Hofsjökull and the sun shone upon it making of it a brilliant white streak, shimmering and shining, beckoning like Lorelei the siren. That she was female there could be no doubt, for what male could possess such beauty; and she called men throughout time, called them to partake of her . . . and some she called to pay the courtesan's price for all.

The sky closed in again. The show was over. It began to rain. The track now turned steeply downhill. There was a clear-watered stream, the headwaters of the great Skjálfandafljót river of the previous two days. It was yet young and had not attained the stately dignity of its maturity. Down amongst lava rocks it bounced and played and was happy in its youth.

Mid-morning showed me another track branching off to the right, tyre-marks churning in all directions like demented python duets. If one were to go down it for a hundred miles or so then one would arrive at the north coast. I had no desires in that direction so continued along my chosen, identical track, down further into Sprengisandur. The wind was gleeful and increased its power to torment . . . like a cat tormenting a mouse.

It was near to this track that almost a hundred years previously a remarkable journey had taken place. Some twenty miles to the north-west stood the farm of Tjarnir, the farm furthest up the Eyjafjarðara river which empties into the Arctic Ocean. At the farm worked the young shepherd Kristinn Jonsson who, early in the morning of September 27th, 1898, mounted and with two companions, left Tjarnir to bring home the sheep for the winter. It was their intention to return that evening so they had with them neither warm clothing nor food. They rode onto the plateau south-east of the valley and, leaving their horses to rest, set off in different directions to search out the sheep. A dense cloud engulfed them and they turned for their horses, but Kristinn, completely disoriented, went in the opposite direction continuing south-east away from the horses and the sheltering valley. He was dressed in a light coat, with a cap upon his head and a pair of very old and worn hide boots beneath which, fortunately, he had two pairs of socks.

Some time later he came to a stream. He knew then that he was lost for had he been going in the right direction there would have been no stream. He decided to stick to the stream hoping that it would lead him to habitation, but possibly because many plateau streams flow so slowly that their direction is undetectable, he unfortunately set off upstream towards the interior of Sprengisandur.

All that night he walked through the cloud, his direction determined by the stream. Having no food he had only the stream itself for sustenance. Next morning he arrived at the source of another river, unbeknownst to him the most northerly tributary of the great Thjórsá river which flows into the North Atlantic south-west of Iceland. Still hoping to find habitation he followed this stream to the south-west and, as it grew dark again, he lay down to sleep in the shelter of a rock. He had been walking for thirty-six hours.

Though it was extremely cold the temperature remained above freezing and after what must have been an extremely uncomfortable night, his collar turned up against the elements, he awoke to find the cloud lifted and to the west, covering almost the whole horizon, an enormous glacier, which he did not know to be Hofsjökull.

He was now convinced that he had gone towards the south, but considered that if he retraced his steps north he would probably become lost or simply die from exposure before he made it. So, shaking the stiffness from his limbs, he continued downstream, convinced that he would eventually find human settlement, not realising how distant that settlement was to be.

All that cold day he followed the stream, crossing tributary after tributary, soaking wet in the desert wind, his strength ebbing with every hour and every step. He refused to give up. By evening, his third on Sprengisandur, the stream had become a substantial river and the glacier was close by to the north. He lay down and slept a short sleep of utter exhaustion, then stood and again continued south-west beside the great River Thjórsá. Kristinn was a Christian man and spoke long and hard to his God, but in the knowledge that God helps those who help themselves he set his mind to the business of survival and walked on. Hunger had left him, as it does, but he was constantly thirsty and drank deeply of the freezing river. Once he came across the tracks of horses, which brought strength to his weakening spirit, but they were old tracks left when the shepherds had driven their sheep to the valleys. He slept that night without shelter and exposed to the wind.

On the morning of the fifth day panic and despair descended upon him. He shouted into the desert the cry of the shepherd as he calls his sheep. 'Haa – aa -- aa!' went his cracked voice, long and distant over the damp dunes of sand, but the only reply was the rush of the desert wind. Alone, he was, and responsible for his own salvation. He fought down the panic, threw away his despair, and continued along the swift-flowing river, walking automatically, one foot before the other, through the clear and frosty desert.

That night he found a shepherd's hut, used when they gathered the sheep, and there he spent the night. There was a frost. By morning there was no feeling in his feet and his hands were blue. The sixth day was again clear and sunny and the resultant beauty of the shining river brought new life to Kristinn. Later that day he saw a magnificent snow-capped mountain to the south-west beyond the river, the volcano Hekla. Ahead was a smaller mountain, Burfell, shining in the distance. He made for it. The desert had gone and grass was under his numb and swollen feet. Before he reached Burfell night closed in again and he collapsed onto the grass. He slept little because of a biting wind and was very close to death. Had he succumbed to despair at this point he would probably have died. This was on his mind during the waking periods of the night as he contemplated his mother's grief and refused to die. However, on the morning of the seventh day, his only hope was to find people so that they could bury him and tell his mother what had happened to her son.

Gathering last remnants of strength, he pulled himself upright and managed to stagger a short distance to a small wood in the shadow of Burfell. There he collapsed and, as he fell asleep, accepted that death was now inevitable.

Incredibly he awoke the next morning and, warmed by the sun, tried to continue. It was hopeless. He collapsed, and there he lay in complete lethargy for some hours. But the spirit of self-preservation is a mighty spirit and again he stood and looked about him. His heart must have danced as he saw, just outside the wood, a few horses casually grazing. He tried to reach them but his legs would not obey his indomitable spirit. There was no-one to be seen. As he finally decided to lie down and wait, a man appeared beside him.

They took Kristinn Johnsson to safety. Unfortunately he lost all of his frost-bitten toes to amputation, but after several weeks he recovered and returned home to Tjarnir, to tell the incredible tale of how he beat Sprengisandur to his mother, his kith and his kin.

Kristinn's route was roughly the route I would be following for the rest of the day; the same damp black sand, the same wind, the same chill of the air. Sometimes it rained and sometimes it did not. Sometimes the wind was strong; sometimes it blew stronger. The cloud-base descended so that sometimes I walked through cloud and sometimes beneath it. It was a cold, wet, miserable trudge with only the thought of the hut ahead to hold onto and preserve some sense of sanity. 'Eff – eye – eff – eye – eff – eye – eff,' I told myself as I imagined the hut coming nearer and nearer with every 'eff' and every 'eye'. About this hut I knew nothing. Was it a hostel, warm with a fire and a warden, with dry beds and a place to cook; or was it a small, draughty, earthen-floored room like my previous temporary home beyond the lava desert so long ago? How long ago? I asked myself. I worked out the happenings since then, counting off the days on my fingers. Only four days? Surely not! I checked my map and confirmed my findings. Yes, four days, and this was the fifth. It seemed so remote in the past, like a piece of history held onto by dimming memories conjured up by marks on paper. I sifted through these memories, idly reinforcing them, anything to take my mind from the featureless nothingness about me.

> *Sprengisandur – Sprengisandur.*
> *Pain in the arse-hole, Sprengisandur!*

It was early evening when I hit the river. Wide it was, about two hundred yards to the far shore. The map designated this point as a ford, and indeed vehicle tracks vanished into the water, each pair at its own chosen point. There were small elongated islands of black sand surrounded by swirling soupy waters, some branches obviously quite shallow but others deep and menacing, running in spate to my right and gurgling meaningful threats. I put on my overtrousers and gaiters, tying them tightly in place. They would keep out some of the water. Then I unstrapped my ice-axe, new and gleaming, two feet nine and a half inches long from its silver steel head, along its red metal shaft to its sharp steel spike, like a hi-tech slim-line mattock. This was the first time I had ever used an ice-axe, and not a bit of ice in sight. It would be useful to judge the water's depth, and as a walking-stick, a third point of contact with the river-bed. Here was a great danger. The power of moving water is phenomenal; and this was flood-water, the collected rains of days.

'No heroics!' I told myself aloud. I noticed the sound of my heart pounding in my ears as a tinge of fear set the adrenalin in motion. There was a debate about whether I should leave my rucksack's waist-strap undone to help me get rid of its dead weight should I fall, or strap it tight to make it more manageable and thus decrease the likelihood of a disaster. I decided upon the latter, taking comfort from the quick-release buckle on the strap. I fastened the strap and pulled it tight, then tested the release, once . . . twice . . . three times so that my hand would know exactly where it was should it need to. My Lancastrian cloth cap I stuffed into my pocket for safety, and I pushed back my hood from my ears for I needed every sense to be as sharp as possible for the coming battle. There was a hairless diabolic presence somewhere in those waters.

'Right!' I said to the absent world and, treading in a few inches of water, leaped a deeper bit to land on a shallow area and step onto the first island. So far so good. The next bit was wider and deeper. A couple of deep breaths and I entered the water heading for the next island, twenty feet away. The first step took the water to my ankle, the second to my lower calf and the third almost to my knee. The water pushed and heaved at me, trying to knock me over. I felt its coldness as it found crevices in my waterproofs and trickled into my boots. I poked ahead, carefully, with my ice-axe and it almost vanished before it hit bottom. I was less than half-way to the island and to take another step would have been madness. The weight of water would have whipped me away like a leaf and if I didn't lose my life I would almost certainly lose my equipment. I retreated, carefully, feeling for solid footing before transferring weight.

Several times I tried, up and down the river. Once I almost reached half-way, and twice I was nearly flung into the waters, but it was hopeless. Common-sense had to win the day. Already I had risked more than I should have. There was no point in trying again.

There were two possibilities. I could either go left and upstream towards Tungnafellsjökull, the steep-sided mountain close by but unseen in the cloud, or wait for a truck to ferry me over this obstacle. I was only three miles from the enigmatic hut and there were two of these fords between me and it. The light was beginning to fade and I was soaking from the knees down. I sat on my pack, exhausted, and peeled off wet boots, socks and overtrousers, wringing out what could be wrung out and emptying what could be emptied.

I had just replaced boots and socks, somewhat drier, when a huge army-type truck came out of the gloom. The driver offered me a lift and I accepted, piling myself into the back which was full of equipment and people. We ploughed through the river as if we were crossing the road, went down the track a while, splashed through another river and stopped. I jumped out, the people waved and the truck vanished into the mist. The whole thing had taken a very few minutes.

There were three huts, two large and one small, each with a brilliant red roof sloping to shed snow and rain. Their wooden structure was quite new and there was an air of almost military efficiency about the place. It had begun to rain again and the wind lashed it against my cagoul. I hefted my sack and walked towards the buildings. The small one was a place of ablution, symbols of a male and a female each on a door. One of the larger huts had a small porch and on an adjacent window the legend 'INFORMATION' in big, black, amateur letters on a piece of paper taped inside the glass. Beyond I glimpsed a light.

I entered the porch awkwardly with my bulky load and gratefully clicked the door closed against the elements. There were boots, scarred, wet and used, around the edge of the floor. Beyond another door was a hall-way with several mysterious doors around it, a rack containing more boots and a table with a visitors' book. On the walls were maps and notices advertising faults and virtues. It was warm. One of the mysterious doors opened and a young, slim and pretty lady, encased in practical wool and denim, came through it. Her blonde hair, obviously long, was tied up conveniently behind and her blue, intelligent eyes, provost-neutral, gave nothing away. She took charge of me.

'Good evening!' she said in clipped, northern-vowelled English. It was as much a statement of fact as a greeting and had I been the weather I would not have argued.

'Good evening,' I replied with a smile, which she returned with her mouth but not with her eyes. She saw the Union Jack on my rucksack, which I had heaved to the floor.

'Are you English?' she asked. No foreigner has ever asked me if I am *British*.

'Yes. From the north of England – Manchester.' I waited for the usual questions about Manchester United and a string of ball-kickers about whom my knowledge is non-existent. She simply nodded, signifying that the information had been stored. I was relieved.

'Are you walking?' she wished to know.

'No, I am resting,' I replied with a grin. It was the best attempt at camaraderie that I could manage as I stood in my widening pool of water. For a brief moment her eyes joined mine in a chuckle, then the barriers went up again. Unbidden, in my mind's eye, a winged helmet appeared upon her head, a shining shield adorned her left forearm and a gleaming sword flashed in her right hand. Wagnerian sounds surged through the cathedral vaults of mind to accompany this Valkyrie of Sprengisandur. From that moment on I thought of her as *Val*.

'You can sleep in *there*,' said Val, pointing at a door with her sword. '*Here*,' again the pointing, 'is the kitchen. There is warm water and plates. You must supply your own gas. *Clean* everything when you have used it. You must take off your boots *here*. You may dry your clothes in the room or in the kitchen. The toilet is *outside*. You must wash at the *toilet*. How long will you stay?'

My head was reeling. 'Maybe two days,' I said quietly. Val nodded. The interview was over. I had been dismissed. I picked up my rucksack and, opening the sleeping-room door, made to enter.

'*Your boots!*' said Val. She didn't shout. In fact she spoke quite softly; but with all the authority of Montgomery at El Alamein. I mumbled apologies and did as I was told.

Inside the room was even warmer with the tang of burning coal in the air and faint crackling sounds coming from an iron stove by the door. Socks and jeans hung sadly from string above it, gently steaming. Around the walls were polished pine two-tier bunks with mattresses and the centre of the long room was taken up by a huge pine table with chairs around. Some of the bunks contained sleeping-bags and other equipment. One sleeping-bag contained a sleeping body. The place was spotless and all was order.

Two young men were eating at the table; one big and well built, the other slim and wiry. We exchanged friendly greetings in English. Everyone in Iceland speaks initially in English. It is the most likely language to be understood by the traveller. I found a bottom bunk in the far corner where I should be least disturbed by the passage of others, decanted and unrolled my sleeping-bag as a sign of occupation, and gathering my cooking equipment and food, padded stocking-footed to the kitchen where there was another stove and more drying clothes. There was a table running around three walls with small collections of stoves, food, pans and other paraphernalia stacked neatly and separately along its length. I found a space and laid claim to it by depositing my own collection. I soon had a hot meal prepared, my first palatable meal for two days. It was good to feel the warmth within join the warmth without. Val entered, minus her militaria but with a gas-lamp which she hung aloft to dispel creeping dark. As I was boiling more water for a cup of good English tea the two young men from the dormitory came in, brandishing dirty plates for the sink. The slim one looked sadly at the flickering flame of my solid fuel and insisted that I use their gas stove, an offer which I couldn't refuse as I was becoming low on fuel.

The big man was an engineer from the Ruhr and the other a Swiss student. They had met in Iceland and were travelling together in loose association for it is pleasant to share holiday experiences with one of like mind. Theirs was a casual journey of a few weeks travelling by foot and whatever transport manifested. They had been to Mývatn and we talked of flies whilst I made my tea, its deep amber oozing from the tea-bag to be joined by sugar and powdered milk in my pint plastic mug.

'Tea?' enquired The Engineer. 'Have you no coffee?' It was said with the smile of banter.

'I am an Englishman!' I said, with a grin, and a finality implying that this was explanation enough.

'I too drink tea,' said Slim, 'and I am Swiss!'

We laughed easy laughter together and I revelled in the welcome pleasantness of friendly relaxation. This was, I reflected, the first time since leaving Manchester two weeks previously that I had held anything but a utilitarian conversation with anyone. I could feel the tensions gathered over the days flowing away with each free and easy word. We are, despite our jealous individualities, remarkably gregarious animals. There was laughter at the slightly discoloured lukewarm water which Slim claimed was *tea*, and at the chicory-smelling fluid which The Engineer's packet designated as *coffee*. They tried my concoction and grimaced to great depths. There was a tranquillity in that warm kitchen as the sky dimmed and the banter evoked honest chuckles out of all proportion to the quality of rhetoric.

Others arrived, mostly Germans and Swiss, and gave stories of flooded rivers. One Swiss, an adventurous white-collar worker with a penchant for survival literature, told of three men very recently drowned nearby when their car was overturned whilst fording a river.

'It was a glacier burst,' he said, warming his hands on a mug of hot soup.

'What is a glacier burst?' I asked, for I had much to learn about this land. He explained that sometimes a lake of meltwater will build up on a glacier. If the lake becomes big enough, often as a result of volcanic activity, it will actually wrench the glacier itself from the underlying rock and rush out beneath the ice in a great flood of power. These bursts are unpredictable in time, place and strength, and can carry away farms and whole communities. I mentioned my plans for Hofsjökull to him and he slowly shook his head.

'It will be very dangerous. There are many rivers to cross, and much strong water. I would not try it.'

The map confirmed what he said. It seemed that even in perfect conditions I could not hope to arrive dry at the glacier, and conditions were about as bad as they could be for the time of year. The recent slackening of tension was reversed as I once more grappled with the problems of the trip. I distinctly remember my jaws being tightly clenched as I drifted off into uneasy sleep.

6   The Glacier

Cold and livening was the morning breeze on my face as I stepped out of the hut. It was just after nine and my rucksack, devoid of all but survival essentials for a day's walk plus my cameras and tape-recorder, weighed a mere twenty pounds or so which, compared with my normal load, seemed like nothing at all.

After much pondering I had decided not to try for Hofsjökull because of the flooding. Word of another death, a lone walker crossing a river, had reached us over the radio. Hofsjökull might well have been possible, I had concluded, but not in the time available. There were only two weeks remaining before I must be in Reykjavik for my plane. So I strode upstream towards the adjacent Tungnafellsjökull, its five-thousand-foot summit a little over five miles east and more than three thousand feet up. I had promised myself a glacier, and this was the nearest.

My compromise glacier was a steep-sided table roughly eight miles by five with its longest axis from south-west to north-east and topped by a white tablecloth of glacial ice. The cloud base had risen to just about the height of the summit which, because I was so close to the mountain, was hidden by the table's edge. My route was to be along the river valley south-west of the mountain for four miles, and thence up gentle slopes to the ice. There were two objectives; the first, a couple of hot springs south of the mountain, and the second, if weather and circumstances seemed feasible, the summit itself. The latter objective seemed a little ambitious and unlikely as I had only book-knowledge of glaciers, but at the very least I wanted to try my crampons on ice and to poke my ice-axe into hard snow.

Before leaving the hut I had done the right thing by telling Val where I was going in case I didn't come back, a sensible precaution in case of injury for to survive even one wounded night on the glacier, cold beyond belief, would be made easier by the knowledge that someone knew roughly where I was and would do something about it in the morning.

The river was to my left and would soon have to be crossed. Still in flood, it was split into numerous rivulets across the flat valley floor. I continued upstream considering that the further I went the less water I would have to contend with. A wall map in the hut had shown a footpath along the valley, but it was just a paper path. There was nothing on the land, soggy and lichen-greened. The valley sides became higher and steeper, and long tongues of black-flecked snow hung down water-courses trying to lap at the river. There came a point where the river touched the base of the right-hand slope, which was now virtually a slag cliff, and passage was halted. The water was perhaps a foot and a half deep and eight feet across to a long island. Swiftly it went, but not too menacingly. I thought of gaiters and overtrousers but considered them superfluous for this initial jump. Finding a good place I leaped, flew and landed with nothing more than a little splashing. The next few leaps were similar and there was soon but one stream to go. It was very slightly wider, and only a little deeper and swifter than the others. Since I knew that I had reached my limits with my previous conquests it seemed that the thing to do was to throw my rucksack across and leap unburdened. Again I disdained waterproofs, elated as I was by success. My cameras were in the flap pocket atop my rucksack so with great care I dispatched it by air across the divide, taking care that it should land on its base where there was nothing to break. I watched in horror as it slowly turned of its own volition, some five feet above the waters, and came

to earth solidly with its base in the air. The crack of its landing
seemed to echo down the valley. Thoughts of a loose
assortment of camera components rattling in a bag passed
through my troubled mind. I ran and leaped into disaster
number two as my foot pierced the water several inches from
the bank and I landed amid an enormous plume of water,
soaked to the skin from the chest down. Mumbling 'Damn!',
and 'Blast!', or words to that effect, I unzipped my camera
pocket. The zip disintegrated. I checked my cameras and took
some shots. Everything seemed to be in order. To say that I
was relieved would be massively to understate my feelings.
The film in my movie camera ran out and required renewing.
Unfortunately in so doing I neglected to flick a crucial switch
which would hold the film behind the lens in its place of focus
and as a result every single frame taken on the glacier was
useless. I was not aware of this at the time of course, and only
discovered my mistake when the film was processed in
England; so, wringing out my jeans and socks I gaily strolled
along the valley taking pointless sequence after pointless
sequence, blissfully happy in my total ignorance of the
situation.

By eleven-thirty I had crossed five tributaries of the river
with little incident, and found myself at the head of the valley.
It was quite warm there, and sheltered from the wind. Twice
the sun had shone through the thinning cloud enabling me to
shoot much better quality rubbish. A small snow-field
punctuated the valley's end, remnant of the previous winter's
hardships. The river running beneath it had carved beautiful
snow grottoes covered by gleaming white bridges fifteen feet
above the water. It was tempting to cross the river by these
bridges, but much damage could be done in a fifteen-foot fall
so I crossed the bubbling waters by stepping from stone to
stone.

Beyond the snow the river rushed from the heights through
a gorge which vanished round a right-hand bend. My route to

the hot springs lay up a steep ridge, not technically difficult but energy-consuming, to the tops. Half an hour later I dragged myself onto a snow-flecked plateau, puffing and panting like a beached grampus. The sun greeted me in splendour, lighting theatrically as magnificent a view as I have ever beheld. The valley of my recent passage stretched two thousand feet beneath me, its green and black floor decorated with the tinsel of moving waters, whilst beyond, fully twenty miles distant, the brilliant whiteness of Hofsjökull stretched evenly in a shallow curve from edge to remote edge, like the upturned dinner-plate of Oðin. It was the kind of sight that can burst a man's heart with the gladness of living.

I stayed a while, then continued on my search for the hot springs. According to the map they were about three miles east of me, amongst a number of sharp needle-point peaks which were difficult to relate to the map owing to their abundance. I hit a snow-field, hard-packed and slippery. This was what my crampons and ice-axe were for. The crampons fitted snugly to my boots, their straps binding them tight, each with ten steel one-and-a-half-inch spikes pointing downwards, and two forward for the steeper slopes. Their weight was noticeable, but not uncomfortable, and it was satisfying to feel the spikes crunch solidly into the crystalline snow, bending at their hinges for ease of walking. My ice-axe, its sling around my right wrist, bit into the whiteness with the sharp spike on the end of its shaft as I walked, slowly at first, then with greater confidence, over the brilliant icy expanse, looking for slight discolorations or unexplained hollows which could denote hidden spaces beneath; spaces that could so easily become a hidden tomb for a broken body. Old Baldie, my companion-in-adversity, was around.

For over an hour I searched diligently for those hot springs, but found them not. Perhaps they were over the next ridge; perhaps to the left. It was not easy to decide with conviction which identical peak was which from the array of points piercing the sky. That sky was murky and the cloud-base very near. It was about two o'clock and if I was to try for the summit then now was my last chance to make that decision. It lay roughly five miles north over what appeared on the map to be some pretty rough terrain. The hot springs or the summit? No contest! I turned my back on the next ridge and walked north, my boots crunching a slow, deliberate rhythm across the snow and ice granules, glittering like a carpet of finely cut diamonds underfoot.

Half an hour later, my spikes and axe stowed, I sat upon a rock overlooking the river which, at that altitude, was in a steep gully. Mouth full of salami and archaeological bread I reflected upon the demeanour of such great men as Nansen, Livingstone, Mallory and Wymper, the heroes of a bygone age. Theirs were names which, in my childhood mind, I had found it difficult to fully separate from those of Superman, Batman and Captain Marvel. They were comic-book heroes who lived in well-bound tomes rather than sixpenny magazines. So far above us common mortals were they that they were as untouchable and unreal as gods. Time and experience had taught me that they were as human as are we, but this knowledge had increased rather than diminished my admiration. They had not possessed the legs of Superman, nor could they have been devoid of fear. True, they were men whose next and subsequent meals were assured when in the country as a whole this was not the case, but they had risen above even their peers into history. What was it that had placed them in this position? What was it that had made them cease to *wish* and strive to *do* the things that were said to be impossible? I concluded that it was an inbuilt insolence which fuelled an outrageous audacity. This was what enabled men with perfectly ordinary bodies, doubtless plagued by rheumatism, athlete's foot and piles, to push back the frontiers of achievement and knowledge for a staid and strait-laced world.

Shackleton was, of course, the exception. He was undoubtedly from the planet Krypton and in his alias was the
father of Clark Kent.

Finishing my meal and washing it down with clear
mountain water I slid down the gully to cross the river. The
climb out was slippery with almost as much back-sliding as
progress; almost, but not quite. Finally I reached the top and
found another snow-field, and another, and yet another. All
in all there wasn't as much snow as I had expected. It lay in
great patches, each about a quarter of a mile across so that I
became quite adept at putting on and taking off crampons.

At three-twenty I found myself at the base of a minor
summit, a perfect cone of volcanic slag about a hundred feet
from base to apex. The sun was shining from a blue-streaked
sky still largely filled with rolling clouds which threatened at
any moment to descend and blot out all vision. The main
summit, on a rocky ridge emerging from the surrounding
snow and ice like a mighty surfacing whale, was over two
miles away and tinged by falling cloud. There seemed a
good possibility that I would not make the ridge in good
visibility, but at that moment the air was as clear as a bell. I
decided to nip up the cone and snap a few shots whilst I
still could.

From the top the view was awesome in its grandeur. To the
west Hofsjökull was obscured by intervening ridges. In the
south-west rose the flat-topped cones of two volcanoes, stark
and black against the sky, whilst north lay the summit ridge.
But it was from the south to the east that the show really took
place. It was white, and went on forever. Vatnajökull, the
biggest glacier anywhere after Antarctica and Greenland, held
splendid court. I could hear, through the biting wind,
Vaughan Williams's *Sinfonia Antartica* accompanying the
vastness of it all, a vastness difficult to comprehend. Great
enough, it was, to create its own weather systems. Clouds cast
moving shadows over its surface, each chasing another, dis-

colouring its brilliant virginity as it said to the world in a voice devoid of pitch, tone or volume '. . . I AM . . .'

For posterity I took some photographs which I knew would be as far removed from reality as snaps of some great and meaningful ceremony are from the partaking. For good measure I destroyed thirty feet or so of perfectly good movie film, unaware of the sacrifice I was making to the great pagan god before me.

Time was a-wasting so I set out once more for the summit, elated by my sight of Vatnajökull. So elated was I that I burst forth, full-lunged, into a yodelling song. There is nothing like a good yodel, and that was *nothing* like a good yodel. My enthusiasm was dimmed when I saw cloud begin to obscure the summit ridge.

At four-thirty I stood at the edge of Tungnafellsjökull's glacier. It barred the way to the ridge. It was white. It was frighteningly, funereally, silent. For over sixteen million years ice had flowed here, flowed a foot nearer to the sea for every day that passed, until it reached a warmer altitude at the snout from where it continued its journey as meltwater. As quickly as it flowed from the mountain it had been replenished by snow, and rain, and mist, so that never throughout the entire history of mankind had it ceased for a moment to grind its inevitable way down the valley. From my right it flowed imperceptibly down a shallow slope to fall to my left into a grim canyon. Long parallel crevasses gashed the surface, narrow to the right but gaping wider as the slope steepened, like a gigantic well-grilled cod separating into gleaming segments. It was two miles and maybe two hours to the summit, most of it over the glacier. If I made it to the summit it would not be much before eight o'clock when I stood again where I now was, leaving me little over a couple of hours of dusk to get off the mountain and into the valley where I would have a comparatively safe walk back to the hut. That was cutting it fine. Also this was my first glacier. True, I knew the theory, but somehow book-learning seemed utterly inadequate now that I was confronted with the real thing. To augment my problems the clouds looked ominously low and threatening. The sensible thing to do was to turn back and try again upon the morrow, but if I had been sensible I would have gone to Blackpool. All manner of reasons came to me for going back, but *there* was the summit within my grasp. In two hours I could be standing on Tungnafellsjökull having beaten my first glacier. The excuses were still going through my head as I buckled the last tight strap on my left crampon and set it firmly, not without trepidation, upon the ice.

I remembered my thoughts as I had lain in my sleeping-bag in Seyðisfjörður: '. . . gamble . . . death for loser . . . achievement for victorious . . . proper caution . . . odds in my favour . . . must not be stupid . . . sound judgement. . .' I was walking a tightrope between the possible and the impossible, and must not allow myself to fall. And Old Baldie was more than willing to shake the rope.

Carefully I poked at the hard snow surface with my ice-axe, thrusting it down to seek for hidden crevasses. At this time of year the crevasses should not be hidden, but open to view, their snow-bridges having melted and fallen, but I was taking no chances. Poke . . . step . . . poke . . . step . . . poke . . . went the rhythm. Slowly the black, solid ground receded like a shoreline; fifty yards . . . a hundred yards . . . two hundred yards . . . the feeling of exposure was tremendous and I have rarely felt so vulnerable. A patch of discoloured snow was ahead, perhaps indicating a void beneath its crust. I avoided it, keeping the odds in my favour. To my right, five feet away, was a narrow crevass, a mere six inches wide. It was a new thing and I was very wary of it. More appeared to the right and left. All the while I was speaking into my tape-recorder, like Armstrong on Luna, talking my way through the unknown.

'. . . Seems pretty solid up to now . . . It's all on a slope . . . I'm doing all the right things . . .'

I wanted to move up the slope to my right so I had to cross the crevass. To step over such a crack in the ice was a fearsome thing. It was only six inches wide, but its depth was unknown. Would the ice on each edge hold my weight, or would it collapse, throwing me down into the ice there to be tightly wedged until the cold drew life from my body? Then the body would begin its sedate two-mile funeral procession down the valley until, thirty years later and perfectly preserved, it would be deposited in the meltwaters at the snout.

I poked the ice at the edge of the gash. It seemed solid enough. There was only one way to find out. The voice of a child, a voice of long ago, rang in my brain amid pictures of paving-stones. 'Don't step on the cracks, or the Devil'll get ya!' Taking a couple of deep breaths I stepped over the edge of the crack. As I passed over it I looked down. Its straight white sides, translucent at the top, gradually became grey where the light dimmed and there was no visible bottom. My crampon spikes crunched welcomingly on the far side and I was over. I was now a qualified crosser of crevasses.

Several others I had to cross, gradually getting wider. I found that with a shambling trot I could manage a two-foot gap. Anything bigger and my bottle went. One or two were over three feet so I stalked along the edge until they narrowed to my specifications. Below and to my left they widened to ten feet and more, not in my league at all.

I was about three hundred yards from the far 'shore' at its nearest point. The hard snow gave way to a glistening ice sheet, good and solid under my spikes. The wide crevasses were behind me as I came, slowly and with much acquired confidence in my new skill, towards the rocks. Then there was solid ground beneath me. I noticed my heartbeat in my ears, pounding and pumping strongly and rapidly. Looking back over the glacier gave a great feeling of elation as I realised that it was beaten. There was now just a mile or so of perfectly ordinary snow to traverse, along the edge of the summit ridge, and then a short scramble to the top. I grinned with happiness and relief.

The walk along the ridge base was straightforward, like a lap of honour. Soon I was below the summit and removing my crampons. That ridge was made of black cinders, crunching and abrasive, breaking with ease so that progress was painful and slow; but eventually I stood on the ridge. The cloud which had been threatening to engulf the summit now did so. In seconds visibility was reduced to a few feet. Very cautiously I picked my way along the knife-edge ridge towards the unseen cairn of stones, impatiently awaiting its appearance and even doubting my direction when, on a couple of occasions, the ridge pointed down and not up.

Suddenly, there it was, the summit; just a pile of rocks and a broken wooden marker, but to me at that moment it was the most wondrous sight in the world. *'Tungnafells-JÖKULL!'* I yelled to the universe in unrestrained joy. Here was achievement. Here was something more solid and personal than acclaim. Medals and material wealth could be taken away, but this could not. It was mine to hold forever. I sat upon my vanquished mountain in a private world bounded on all sides by swirling, cold, damp cloud and was deeply, magnificently happy.

It was six o'clock. There were three shots left in my still camera and a few feet of cine film left to ruin. Conditions were such that I did not expect any acceptable results, but one doesn't climb Tungnafellsjökull every day. For twenty minutes I set up cameras and posed gleefully before them, waving the Union Jack and my ice-axe at posterity, then it was time to go. The cloud had thickened and I was late. So I took a deep breath, literally jumped off the side of the ridge, and slid down to the snow.

Here I was below the cloud, but barely. It was coming in like a solid wall down the slope of the glacier. Quickly, and by now expertly, I strapped on my crampons and set out over the snow. I did not follow my tracks along the base of the ridge but set off in a straight line directly across the glacier. I was in a hurry. I was on an unfamiliar mountain and had no faith whatsoever in my compass. The wind direction was erratic so my navigation depended entirely upon visibility. If I could not see the terrain, or at the very least the sun's direction, then I would be lost. To be lost at over four thousand feet in cloud that could last for days would be a very serious business indeed; far more serious than on the moor for there I had full camping equipment whilst here I had only my hooped bivi for an emergency shelter. In the expected sub-zero temperatures, with the dampness of the cloud about, it might or might not save my life. To stumble around in dense cloud with precipices all about was a sure formula for disaster. No, I had to reach the valley before the cloud engulfed me. Old Baldie had a firm hold on my tightrope and was beginning, gleefully, to shake it.

There was no testing of the snow before me now as I almost ran down and across the slope pursued by the advancing cloud. Every sense was alert as I took great strides over the pristine whiteness. Soon I was amongst the crevasses. I leaped one, and another; several gashes two and even three feet wide I shambled to and leaped, trotting awkwardly in my crampons. And still the cloud came on, silent and billowing like steam from some mighty kettle. It was about seven when I gained the solid land again and removed my spikes. I was at a different place from where I had stood before. Here the ground was broken and traversed by deep ten-foot gullies of breaking cinders. Up and down I scrambled, going ever south towards the river valley, not caring to look for the route I had taken to the top. It was three miles to the valley, and daylight was beginning to fade. I hit a snow-field, quite shallow in its slope with no visible cliffs to fall over should I slip. Leaving my crampons strapped to my rucksack I walked rapidly and carefully over it heading south . . . south . . . south. There were my previous tracks, a lonely dotted line crossing my path. I ignored them and continued on my line of march. Several snow-fields later, at about eight o'clock, there was a definite line to the edge of the snow ahead. The cloud had overtaken me and sought to smother me, swirling and eddying about and above. To the edge I came, and sure enough the ground dropped rapidly down to the silver-streaked dark valley below. The snow ran down a very steep gully in liquid form, cascading over rocks and gurgling through cracks. That way was too steep and broken for safety but there seemed to be a gentler way to the left which I took. Down, down I went, below the cloud once more, dislodged rocks bouncing and rattling down the steep slope to the flat land two thousand feet below. Old Baldie still clutched the tightrope . . .

The cold evening wind lulled as I went lower into the valley's shelter. My immediate enemy was no longer the cloud but the encroaching darkness. The valley was deep and would blot out all the glow of the night-time sun. Already it was past eight o'clock and the river had become indistinct. I had perhaps an hour of any kind of light remaining. The way down was steep and precarious. Several times I had to retreat from sheer cliffs, edging my way carefully over the loose rock and shale. Sometimes I was amongst boggy patches clinging and festering in little incongruous niches. Often I slipped and clawed at crumbling rocks for purchase, once or twice above precipices of sheer rock a hundred feet and more deep.

Below me was the narrow ravine along which flowed the river. It was black and mysterious, but the quickest way down seemed to be into it. Normally the rule is to stay out of ravines as one can become trapped, but time was short and sometimes one must take a chance. Down I went, cascading rocks before me, until I stood on boulders beside the rushing river. It was fifteen feet wide and hurrying down towards the wide valley as if it, too, were scared of the dark. The sound of its passage echoed in the narrow confines as I leaped from rock to rock along the narrow defile. The sides became sheer rock walls and the passage became narrower, a thin streak of darkening sky above. Suddenly, unannounced, the river leaped over a shelf and fell for ten feet or so between smooth pillars of rock into a deep pool. That was it! I could not continue in anything like safety so I had to retrace my steps back to where I had come down to this narrow dungeon. You win some ... and some you undoubtedly lose.

The scramble out was difficult, up crumbling rocks, slipping on moss and lichen, moving on against the inexorable enemy. There were a couple of nerve-tingling rocky traverses with dangerous drops should I make a mistake, but soon the ground became gentler and I reached the snow-bridges remembered from that oh-so-long-ago morning. I was on terra-reasonably-firma and it was nine o'clock. Old Baldie was beaten again! In two hours I would be back at the hut some five miles distant, and I had climbed Tungnafellsjökull. I strolled down the gloom-filled valley on the red carpet of euphoria, leaping friendly streams and bouncing over comradely grass. At eleven I reached my major river-crossing. I was utterly fatigued and, knowing that within a very short time I would be warm and dry, simply walked across from island to island, ignoring the liquid content of the intervening areas.

It was pitch-black as I approached the hut. Two large flames marked the spot to guide me home. There were wraith-like figures moving about in their light. Val, Slim and The Engineer greeted me like the prodigal and ushered me to the kitchen, questioning and happy. There was a comforting relief in their faces which spoke of the eternal bond between adventurers. I knew without question that they would have been out before dawn and searching if I had not arrived.

Val ritually admonished my lateness, but there was a softening of her demeanour. We drank warm drinks amid steaming socks whilst I told of my triumph, proudly, to an enraptured captive audience. There was talk that I was almost certainly the first Englishman to solo Tungnafellsjökull across the glacier, perhaps even the first person ever. Whatever the truth of the matter I felt the occasion and had great difficulty manoeuvring my head through the dormitory door when I took my ego to bed.

The Engineer and Slim rose and departed early. With another lady warden to guide them they had set out for Tungnafellsjökull by a different route, shorter and avoiding the glacier, so that when I awoke they were already gone. It was to be for me a day of rest, of stock-taking and of planning. My body, particularly my legs and feet, tingled with the painful fitness of recent exertion such that even to walk to the toilet was an occasion to be planned and worked up to. The sun was splendidly set in a flawless blue sky and the wind had gone. Val said that the forecast was for three more days of this over all of Iceland. It was an unprecedented occurrence in Sprengisandur and she gloated over the radio to colleagues in more amenable postings who had previously expressed sympathy for her banishment whilst holding private relief that it was Val, not them, who must go to the desert. She demanded that the next consignment of groceries should contain quantities of sun-tan oil, then went out to smile at the sun.

  This forecast brought with it a dilemma. My next major challenge, the high-spot of the entire expedition, was the volcano Hekla, two days' hard walking away; two more days over Sprengisandur. Including my day of rest, an absolute necessity, it would mean that I would arrive at the base of Hekla just as the weather closed in again. There was much to consider. To attempt to climb Hekla in bad weather would be madness, and also largely pointless since one of my purposes was to make a film of the trip. To wait for more good weather was out of the question as my aircraft would be leaving for Glasgow in fourteen days, strictly on time. There was a bus coming through the following day which could take me to the base of Hekla with one day of good weather left to climb it, but what of the charity walk, and the sponsorship money promised for every trudged mile? The answer, I concluded, was to shuffle the cards. Hekla was, like Tungnafellsjökull, a side-trip and not part of the actual crossing of Iceland which I had contracted with my sponsors. I would therefore take a three-day holiday from the crossing, use it to climb Hekla, then return to the hut to complete the crossing. Honour and sponsors should then be satisfied and I would have my film. I was happy with that decision and speculated long on the coming climb.

I discovered that my still camera had indeed smashed when I had thrown my bag over the river. It would not wind on. My knowledge of the innards of a single-lense reflex camera was of similar proportions to my knowledge of Manchester United – it's history and development, but drastic circumstances demand drastic solutions. I washed my hands, cleared a space on my bunk, and commenced to explore the mysteries of its internal structure with the aid of My Father's Sword, a procedure akin to conducting brain surgery with an axe. The piles of minute screws, bits of weirdly shaped metal of unknown purpose, and items of electrical circuitry, grew apace, but no progress did I make. Finally I reassembled it in a slightly worse condition than before and took solace in that my movie camera was still intact. I replaced the wasted hundred-foot reel of film with a good one, still not realising the fact of its demise. Up to this point my light-metering for both cameras had been done through my still camera, but the meter, too, was broken. From then on all light entered my movie camera by guesswork, which in the event went very well as I managed to produce some excellent film which was subsequently shown on TV.

In the early evening the alpinists returned, tired and happy, and not a little muddy. They enthused about the view from the summit, one which I would dearly have loved to see.

'It was beautiful,' said the tall and tomboyish guide in quite a deep voice, 'I was very proud.'

Her name was Brynhild the Battle Maiden, I decided. Travellers and associated persons rarely seem to be concerned with each others' true names. We are passing night-ships and such intimacies seem unimportant. The ladies invited us to dinner, a makeshift catch-as-catch-can affair of tinned vegetables, potatoes, bread and boiled sausage which Brynhild, with tongue firmly in cheek, insisted was *horse*. We talked of the Cod War when Iceland had extended her maritime boundaries much to the chagrin of British fishermen. I came to know the position as seen through Icelandic eyes.

'We are fighting for survival!' said Val. 'Fish is all we have. You have many things: coal and oil, and agriculture. We have only the fish; and soon they will be gone.'

'Then we will have only the tourists,' said Brynhild, presenting a united front. I thought of all the new temporary bridges throughout the land, and the new southern coastroad. These were undoubtedly useful for domestic communication, but were mainly a survival strategy aimed directly at tourism.

'Soon we must live on the *tourists*,' confirmed Val.

'Fish tastes better,' I said to inject a little humour into the gathering gloom. It worked, and smiles creased faces. Val had spoken the word *tourists* with utter disdain. We three foreigners knew that this disdain did not extend to us for we were *travellers*, not *tourists*. Always there is this distinction, throughout the world, between the traveller who accepts discomfort in order to *see*, and the tourist who demands all the comforts of home, and looks without seeing. The former are met with varying degrees of acceptance whilst the latter are treated as a necessary evil.

'One German asked when was the season for volcanoes,' said Brynhild, shaking a disbelieving head.

I broached my theory of the proximity of the Icelandic language, Old Norse, to my native Lancastrian, and we agreed that the flat vowels were common to both our enunciations. Some vocabulary remained in common. A *fell* was to us a mountain, and what to the Icelander was a *foss* was to me a *force*, whilst to an English speaker it would be a *waterfall*.

'More *horse*?' asked Val. We demolished the pseudo-equine with relish and gazed through the window at a Land Rover ploughing its cascading way through the waters of the ford, its headlights beaming left and right and up and down in the evening's fade, and its engine screaming and roaring in protest.

'Tourists!' said The Engineer.

'Tourists!' confirmed Slim and myself.

'Yes . . . *tourists* . . .' said Val softly; and Brynhild nodded her head.

7   The Volcano

'Hekla is one thousand, four hundred and ninety-one metres high, or five thousand feet. Its last eruption was three years ago in 1981 and it also erupted in 1980. Hekla may erupt at any time. The land is covered by tephra from these two eruptions. We have with us a traveller who will try to climb the volcano tomorrow.'

The courier smiled at everyone in the bus and replaced her microphone in its clip as the bus slid to a halt on the cinder road. The door opened and the passengers waved and smiled.

'Good luck.'

'I hope the weather stays fine.'

'I hope it does not erupt under you.'

'A safe journey.'

A wave, and the bus was gone, its dust settling back onto the road. I looked to the south. There was nowhere else that it was possible to look for there, eight miles away, was Hekla, like a gargantuan Brazil nut sideways-on with snow on its flanks and a summit crest that one had to pull back one's head to view in comfort. And from the centre of that crest, stilled by size and distance, a neat plume of brown smoke arose in a clean curve to the left and dissipated itself into the darkening blue evening sky. Twice a century it had been wont to erupt, since its first recorded eruption in AD 1104. Twice a century, until in 1980, after only ten years repose, it had blown again; and again the following year. Now it was in uneasy doze. Throughout the ancient world it had been known as the Gate of Hell itself, and the smoke was the collected souls of the dead. None would venture up its slopes, for who would wish to visit Hell before the appointed hour?

For a while I stood, just looking, taking in the sight, remembering the legends, thinking of the morrow. Then I heaved my pack onto my back and went to meet it. First I had to cross the Thjórsá river, a wide and swirling affair. This was no problem since a hydroelectric dam spanned it at this point. Kristinn the shepherd must have stood on this spot a hundred years ago, and three miles to the south-west was Burfell at the foot of which he was found. I exchanged pleasantries with some workmen on the dam and continued on towards the mountain. Crossing the main Sprengisandur road I went east along a narrow unmade road which skirted the north of the mountain, and which led to a possible route up. The map promised an abundance of streams along the track, so I neglected to fill my water-bottle with murky river-water.

The light was fading fast as I followed the road which was deep-gouged and frequently marked by reflector-posts, for this was on the edge of the more populated part of Iceland, the area surrounding Reykjavik some seventy miles away to the west. Sheep showed mild interest as I passed. Once or twice I saw a deep gully and left the road in search of water, but each time there was only tephra, small half-inch black cinders which blanketed everything to a depth of several inches. Occasionally sparse blades of grass would pierce its surface to proclaim the perpetual tenacity of life. Water began to be a problem. My map, I concluded, had been made before the recent eruptions when all streams had, seemingly, been covered by tephra. There was, a mile to the south on the map, a largish circular lake of obvious volcanic origin, so I left the road in its direction. I crunched over an ex-stream-bed and beheld the strangest of sights before me. There, barring my way to the lake, was a forest of stone 'trees' some ten to fifteen feet high. The 'tree trunks' were thick at the base and branched into sharp needle-points at the tips. The forest 'floor' itself was ten feet above the tephra commencing in a definite line of massive, clean-edged boulders. It was an eerie and strangely alien sight, the trees stark against the darkening blue of a sky which was beginning to allow stars to twinkle. I clambered over the boulders to the trees. They were made of lava, turned solid as it seethed and bubbled into the petrifying coolness of the air, there to remain as natural sculptures until time eroded them to dust.

This was *aa* lava, not the flat slabs that had formed the desert cornflakes, but the new lava which Hermann the German had said I might encounter; the lava that would tear my boots apart. This had probably belched out from Hekla in the 1981 eruption and as yet had had no time to erode any of its sharpness. There was no level floor and the trees were close enough together to make one have to select carefully a path possible to squeeze through. The needle-points stabbed the skin, drawing blood, and broke beneath the feet, flinging the unwary against the spikes. It was obviously madness to continue in that light so I retreated to the tephra. A waterless, thirsty night was in prospect, with my next drink probably on the volcano's snows. It was becoming very cold indeed as I unpacked my bivi and set it up on the crunching cinders, hoping that the pegs would have enough purchase to keep it up through the night. Hekla was still lit by the dipping sun, its frozen water tantalising through the petrified forest and looking incredibly, breathtakingly, beautiful.

The boy watched as what had been the old warrior was laid to rest, stiff like a log and dressed for battle, helmet upon proud head and grey beard little disturbed by the breeze. A shield covered the breast and in the right hand, clenched tighter in death than ever in life, was an iron sword scarred by metal and bone. He looked to the horizon where Hekla, the gateway to

Hell, brooded and knew that the old warrior even now stood before the gods in trial. From atop the great mound of Hekla, in a thin grey whisp, arose the souls of heroes bound for Valhalla in Asgard and soon, he hoped, the old warrior would follow.

The goði lifted his arms above the people and intoned words of deep wisdom; the goði who, by common consent, was their leader in all matters sacred and secular, pastoral and martial. Earth showered down upon the remains and was levelled. The place was marked, but the old warrior's body was now a part of the earth, gone from the gaze of men. The boy pondered this a while and turning to the man whose name, perhaps, was Olaf, he asked of the beginning of earth, and of men.

They sat and settled themselves in silence, for this was important work, and the man spoke in the ancient way, as his father, and his father before him, had spoken.

'In the days of long ago, when the gods were young and the clay giant had his being, there were born unto him the evil frost giants. And he the untamed led his sons in conflict against All-father Oðin and the gods of Asgard. The sounds of battle raged for age upon age until the clay giant lay slain. Then the gods flung the body of the giant of clay into Ginnunga-gap and it filled the gap from edge to edge. From a great gash in his neck burst forth a mighty deluge which drowned all the race of evil frost giants save one. He, the wise Bergelmir, built a great boat and saved himself and his wife from the flood. They sailed to the timbers of the mill of the gods, the stones of which rotate about the star of the north, the world spike, and there Loki, the brother of Oðin, gave them refuge, for the mill of the gods is in his charge. And Bergelmir fathered the Jutuns, the evil giants who forever harbour enmity against the gods.

'Then Oðin called the gods together in council, and the council they called the *Thing*. The clay giant, the untamed power of nature, was now tamed by death. Nature must now be shaped and the earth ordered in its ways. They took the body of clay and cast it into the mill of the gods which ground slower than slow and finer than fine. They took the bones and from them built the hills and the mountains, and of his teeth they made the boulders and the pebbles. His flesh they formed into soil, and in the soil they placed growing things which they wove from his hair. And around the lands they placed the rolling oceans which were the sweat of his body. Then they took his mighty eyebrows and from them they fashioned a garden of great beauty to be the dwelling-place of men. His skull they raised and placed over the earth, and from his brain they whisked the clouds to rain goodness upon the land.

'But there was yet no light to bring joy to the world. A few sparks of fire came from Muspelheim, the home of brightness, and wandered aimlessly above the earth. These the gods took and fixed to the skull of the clay giant, and spun the skull slowly around the world spike.

'Now Loki, in whose charge was the mill of the gods, aspired to usurp Oðin. In punishment the gods took his two beloved children and caused them forever to traverse the firmament and to mark the passage of time. To the beauteous Sol they gave a chariot of shining gold drawn by twin horses and made her to race from morn unto evening across the sky. And to her handsome brother Mani they gave a chariot of shining silver drawn by a swift white horse and made him to race from evening unto morn. So it became that nature was ordered in its ways, and that it would ever remain so Oðin placed His beloved wife Frigga to have dominion over it, to tend it and to hold it to her breast, and to be the mother of nature to whom it would go in times of trouble.

'And so it was that one day the mighty brothers Oðin, Hönir and Loki left the great *Thing* council in Asgard to wander along the shores of the beautiful garden of men, which was called Midgard. As they walked they beheld two logs of wood upon the sand. One was of ash, and the other of alder, and they lay lifeless upon the shore.

'Then the mighty Oðin breathed upon them and gave unto each a soul and a mind; and the gentle Hönir touched them and gave unto each motion and senses, and the will to use them; and the powerful Loki caressed them and gave unto each blood and colour, and desire.

'The ash log became man, and his name was Ask; and the alder log became woman, and her name was Embla. And as the times passed they gave birth to all the races of men that roam Midgard with skin of many hues. And when Oðin calls their souls unto Him then they are judged by the gods. The unworthy are given to Hel, the Queen of Hell – the Realm of Torture, there to be punished according to their judgement. And to Hell go traitors and warriors who die without valour; but to those warriors who are valiant Oðin sends his handmaidens, the Valkyries, clad in shining armour, who ride white horses across the sky, flashing in light-clouds as they descend to award the kiss of death and bear their spirits directly to Valhalla. But their bodies must return to the soil from which grew the two logs, that life may be renewed in the great turning of the mighty mill of the gods.'

They walked home, the boy and the man whose name, perhaps, was Olaf; and as they walked, the arm of the man about the shoulders of the boy, they thought, each in his own understanding, of the things that had been spoken; and of the old warrior they thought as Sol dipped her golden chariot towards Hekla, gently smoking in the west.

The silence shook me awake at six. It was an utter silence; a windless, rainless, peopleless silence. I moved and my tephra bed crunched with an alarmingly loud noise. Breakfast was biscuits and chocolate bought from a small shop at a hydroelectric plant late the previous afternoon. There too I had had my last drink, a bottle of gassy, alcohol-free beer. My thirst was strong, but more an annoyance than a danger and I knew I would drink on Hekla.

Loudly I unzipped my bivi. The outside was covered in frost and ice. I sucked a small piece of ice and watched several brazen primates searching diligently for their bearings. The eastern horizon was red as the sun struggled to mount the foothills. The petrified forest brooded coldly thirty feet away, as solid and belligerent as a fortress. Even in daylight, I concluded, that was not for crossing. Quickly I packed up my camp and looked up again. The forest had gone. So had the rest of the world save for a twenty-foot circle around me. Mist, white and thick, cold and damp, blanketed everything. A faint glow showed the direction of the battling sun, so I headed for it to gain the road. It was my wish to set up a base-camp near to that road at a point where I would be sure to find it upon my return from the volcano. As a youth I had learned a hard lesson in Snowdonia when I once left a base-camp in a nondescript field and spent most of the freezing night searching the Llanberis Pass for it. This, I vowed, would not occur again! Such is the arrogance of those who assume aspects of maturity.

The road appeared, and down it I happily strode. Within the hour Sol won her battle and dissipated the mist, warming the land from an almost cloud-free sky. Hekla had become visible and incredibly intimidating, black and white like a piebald pony, a streak of cloud around its feet. A track, barely discernible, went to the right. It was along this track that I wished to go as, according to the map, it would take me to the very base of Hekla. There was a large rock, about twenty feet high, close to the intersection. This looked like a good place for my base-camp. I set up my bivi in a hollow so that it was not visible from the road, thus reducing the possibility of casual robbery. When I found the road, even if I hit it elsewhere, then all I had to do was follow it and look for the large rock. Such was the theory. That was my first mistake.

At eight-twenty I set off down the side-track with a very light load. Even my snow and ice gear, my ice-axe and crampons, I left behind as it was my intention to follow the snow-free north-east ridge to the summit vent. That was my second mistake.

The weather was glorious enough almost to blot out my thirst. Around and about were small petrified coppices of aa lava. There was an extensive forest of stone which pushed the track along the route designated on the map. By this time the track had become very sparse indeed, being simply the odd vehicle track heading roughly in the direction of another. At ten the track met another one, as the map said it should. This second track had greater distinction and took a more direct route to the road. I resolved to use it upon my return. Heklawards I went along it until about forty-five minutes later it ended abruptly as the slope became too steep for it. There was a fresh set of footprints, large and very recent. Within a couple of hours someone had passed this way heading for the mountain.

Then I saw a wonderful thing. A massive block of snow, gleaming white and lonely like Lot's wife. I scrambled up to it and felt its coolness, chipping off a little and sucking it, grit and all, gleeful and happy in the morning. It was a great wedge ten feet high, sticking out of the side of the volcano like the proud prow of a longship, and topped, strangely, with a layer of tephra. I concluded that this snow had fallen in the winter of 1980–81, had been covered by the tephra of the 1981 eruption, and having cooled it, had in turn been insulated by it through the ensuing three years. So there *were* snow-balls in Hell!

There was a point of constant dripping as the sun assailed its pitted east wall. I stuck my cup beneath it and watched it slowly fill with a 'plip-plop-plap'. Out came my cine-camera and I shot an excellent sequence with the lens-cap firmly in place. Ah, the joy and excitement of that hour's rest as I ate and drank my fill, knowing that I felt as Ali Baba must have felt amidst his troglodytic treasure; for here was the most precious treasure of all, here was *water*.

Periodically tephra would fall from the top as the snow beneath it melted. It fell unerringly down my neck until I had the good sense to move out of range. Too soon it was time to go. There was cinder-tasting iced water in my bottle to bring continued happiness. The foothills were steep-sided and covered in tephra. Sometimes the black, crunching cinders would be very deep and my legs vanished to the calves, having to be dragged out with every step. It was reminiscent of aklé dunes in the Sahara, the great crescent barchan dunes of soft, loose sand which gripped the leg and made a penance of progress. But progress there was, and hill after hill was climbed with panting and grunting and blowing, the plain below becoming more distant with each step.

I came to a dusty plateau, other-worldly with strange exploded rocks dotted about its surface, the aftermath of a Hellish battle of fire. These rocks were known as *bombs*. Up to three feet or so in diameter, they had been ejected from the volcano as globules of molten lava, solidified in mid-air and exploded on impact. They were called *bread-crust* bombs because of the appearance of the deep cracks on their surfaces which were reminiscent of the tops of crusty loaves. Tephra lay on them betraying their pre-1981 origin. When the ancients saw such bombs fly out from Hekla's crater they imagined them to be the souls of the damned laid out on the snow by Hel to cool for a while before returning to continue their punishment. The wind blew strongly here and whipped the black dust into wraiths which fled before its might. When I had crossed this barren battlefield I stood, finally, on the shoulder of the volcano itself. It was one-twenty, five hours since I had left my base-camp. There was nowhere else to go now but up.

The shoulder was protected by a stone forest, its trees shorter than the ones below on the plain, but still from five to ten feet high and close-packed. The only way up was through them so I girded my loins and sallied forth somewhat daunted. Progress was very slow indeed. The lava of the desert, which I had considered to be the worst terrain that I had ever encountered, now seemed immensely desirable compared with this passage. To put weight on anything meant a fifty per cent chance of its collapsing, resulting in a fall onto needle-sharp spikes. I shall carry the scars of that journey for many years yet to come. My hands and wrists dripped blood front and back as I struggled through that arboreal lava, snagging straps on branches and gouging deep cuts in stout leather boots, just as Hermann the German had predicted. The forest went sharply uphill and so did I, for how long I do not know. Then I saw a sloping snow-field up a gully ahead, narrow and smooth, and immensely desirable. I went for it, even though I had no snow gear with me. Anything was better than that Hell-forest.

The snow was hard and slippery, speckled with tephra which helped my boots to grip its surface. Very carefully I eased my way up the snow slope, making sure that each foot was firmly planted before bringing up the other. It was hard, and progress was difficult to appreciate, trapped as I was between forests either side and below. I told myself that each footfall was another six inches of the five-thousand-foot total; two steps were a whole foot and six an entire yard.

At the top of the gully the sun had melted great holes in the snow and I was amazed to see, in the snow-cave grottoes, that there were two distinct layers of tephra embedded within the snow. The top layer of white, about a foot thick, must have been from the winter of 1983–84; then a two-inch layer of tephra from the '81 eruption followed by a foot of '80–81 snow below which was '80 tephra. Finally there was a deep layer of snow the top of which could not have been laid later than the '79–80 winter. At least five years of turbulent recent history was here in this pretty party layer-cake in the sky.

There was more deep, steep tephra beyond the snow-field evoking childhood memories of climbing piles of school-yard coke. I chuckled at another early memory of a time when I considered Snowdon to be physically demanding. Ah, the innocence of youth. Another snow-field presented itself, again invisible from the plain below. This was at less of an angle than the previous one as I was considerably further along the crest of the Brazil-nut ridge. I wished that I had brought my crampons and ice-axe; but wishing accomplishes naught save frustration so onward I went as best I could.

There was tephra along the left-hand edge so I followed this a while. Then I saw the large footprints I had seen earlier beyond the foothills. Someone was ahead; perhaps a couple of hours, but no more; someone with big feet, and also without crampons or ice-axe. He too was taking the route along the tephra-strewn edge of the snow. Although he was so far ahead he was like a companion who, though unseen, partook of the difficulties of the day. I had been told that probably ten people per annum climbed Hekla and I was very happy indeed to share the volcano with him.

At two-forty-five I emerged from amongst the lava-trees onto the edge of the main snow-field covering the north-western face of Hekla. The view was magnificent, such as I had seen only from the air. This snow-field, I knew, for I had studied it from below, went for two miles or so below the ridge towards the base of the crater cone. As I looked towards the as yet invisible cone the mighty white sheet fell to the right at a slightly convex 1 in 2, three thousand feet down the mountain; three thousand feet of glistening, smooth, hard, slippery flawless snow with a sharp horizon-like line where it curved beyond vision. The summit-ridge itself was at this point

resplendently 'aforested'. I filmed a little and rested, taking in
the view. Most of the actual climbing was now done, but I
assumed that my problems were far from over. I was right.

Time demanded that I take the route along the upper edge
of the snow rather than tackle the forest. My unseen comrade,
too, had made the same decision and I carefully followed his
lead. An hour later I was over that field and up to the first
summit-vent. There were, along the ridge, not just one crater
but several attendant minor ones in line. I had always imagined volcano craters to be neat and circular, and wasn't
mentally prepared for what I saw. The top of the mountain
had simply burst and great cracks and fissures half-filled with
white brimstone, yellow sulphur, red ferrous cinders and
black tephra, ran in unorganised directions. Mighty slabs of
once-molten rock at crazy angles, jagged and formless,
brooded above and below in diabolical riot as wisps of sulphurous steam wafted, barely visible, in the perceptibly warmer wind. It was a scene impossible to describe, as to do so it
would be necessary to conjure up common experience of that
which has definite form and order. Here was a world un-
formed and orderless. There was no stand-point, no lowest
common denominator, no bottom line from which to begin to
build a description. As even the horizon was blotted out
beyond the mighty monoliths there were no visible horizon-
tals and no verticals; even gravity had doubtful direction as
impossible rock configurations denied its majesty. There was
a word that I had often used glibly to describe disorders
experienced in a largely orderly existence, but whose depths
of meaning, whose essence I had never truly understood until
that moment. The word was *chaos* . . . One thinks of mountains as the epitome of permanence, the perpetual viewers of
the passage of time; but here was the essence of imperma-
nence. Three years previously it had looked nothing like this,
and to put down a foot was to rearrange it once more.
It seemed that the only thing offering any semblance of

permanence was the next snow-field, so in its direction I turned.

Away from the actual geoexplosion the tephra was very thick. Several fissures, some ten feet wide, lay across my route to the snow. They were filled to overflowing with loose tephra and only a sagging of the black, even blanket of cinders indicated their presence. Jumping was out of the question as there was nothing solid from which to take off. I stood up to my knees in tephra and worried. Before me was a tephra-filled chasm, its surface a mere dip, a hollow, which steamed and smoked a little. There was nothing solid beneath that surface for I knew not how far, and it seemed that somewhere down there the tephra was still red hot. The only way to gain the other side was to step into that hollow. 'Oh dear,' I said to myself. 'Oh dear, oh dear, oh dear.'

Taking a deep, sulphurous breath I hesitated almost to the point of being lost, then flung myself at the other side. I sank immediately to my waist in tephra, lay on my belly and swam and clawed my way across the chasm; and I made it. For some minutes I lay there, heart pounding, boots and sleeves and collar full of small prickly cinders. Then I got up and did it again across the next one, and the next, and yet again. Eventually I gained the comparative solidity of the snow and stood on it with relief.

This was the last snow-field. It would take me to the base of the cone. My watch said four-twenty and it seemed that I should not be on top much before six o'clock. This was, as on the glacier, cutting it fine, and the terrain was much worse than on Tungnafellsjökull. But there could be no question of turning back now. I had come to climb a volcano, and climb it I would. Getting down was an entirely different project. If the worst came to the worst I could always hole up until morning. It would be damned cold and uncomfortable but I would survive, and I would have climbed Hekla.

The new snow-field was steeper than the rest, at about

forty-five degrees and slightly convex like a crown bowling green. At its top the heat from the vent had melted back the snow so that a twenty-foot-wide gap separated the top edge of the snow from the cinder wall. The snow curved like a surfing-wave frozen just before it broke on the cone. I had to walk a line atop the crest close to the edge of the overhang where the slope was just gentle enough to walk on; too far to the left and I would fall perhaps fifty feet through the over-hang, too far to the right and I would slide down three thousand feet of slippery snow in about two minutes to be smashed against the first obstacle I encountered. The opti-mum width of this invisible line was probably not much more than a foot. There was no sign of my unseen comrade's pas-sage so I was alone. Very carefully, but not too slowly, I set out about eighteen inches from the overhang's edge.

Sometimes there was an ash-fall rattling to my left, probably dislodged by the wind and reasserting the mountain's im-permanence. Gently, sure-footed, leaving hardly any foot-prints, I crept cat-like along that arbitrary line on the hard, polished snow. Once I dislodged a large cinder which lay on the snow's surface and I watched it bounce down the slope, gathering speed as it went, until it vanished over the half-mile distant clean curve of the snow-field. The wind was strong and steady from directly in front, clean, dry and cold, seemingly coming directly from the dipping, eye-screwing sun.

I slipped – and fell – on my back . . . I slid down the slope . . . I turned over – onto my belly . . . I spread-eagled myself . . . I slid faster . . . I kicked with my boot toes – clawed with my finger-nails . . . I slowed . . . I stopped . . . I lay – still – still – stiller than death – not daring to breathe – fighting the terror – keeping it in its place – thinking – mentally checking each limb for injury – each point of contact with the hard, smooth snow – willing myself to be welded to its surface.

Slowly, carefully, but strongly I scratched out finger-holes with my nails, the warmth of my fingers melting the snow. At the back of my mind was the admonishing thought, '*Crampons! You should have brought crampons!*' But I had not brought crampons. The cardinal rule was *always take crampons and ice-axe.* I didn't think I would need them so I had broken the rule. Now I was paying the price. But the time for recriminations was later. Now I had to get myself out of the mess my foolishness had got me into, or pay the ultimate price of folly.

My finger-holes were big enough to hold me. I raised my head to look up the slope. My slide had taken me only twenty feet or so. It had seemed much, much further. Gripping hard with my fingers I raised myself to my knees, then kicked a toe-hold with my right foot. Very carefully I inched up to the top of the crest like that, using my hands for balance, and perhaps ten minutes later stood gingerly where I had fallen, heart pounding a bone-shaking beat. Then taking a couple of deep breaths I set off once more, even more carefully. It had been a close thing; a very close thing indeed. Yes, Old Baldie was a trier.

There comes a time, some minutes after an accident, when the body, as a result of temporarily overloading the brain, reacts by an almost uncontrollable shaking. As I walked on I noticed this effect beginning to work its way through arms and legs as my heart still hammered my chest with a merciless beat. I should, I told myself, stop to calm myself awhile; but it was late and there was no time for resting. Mind fought brain, slowly subduing. Gradually the shaking stopped and the heart was quieted again as I continued along that invisible pathway atop the snow's overhang.

At four-fifty I was at the base of the cone. The snow ceased and the loose pile of steaming cinders began. It was time to speak to posterity.

'I think I'm on the main cone. There's a lot of steam coming out of the sides of the cone . . . It's beginning to get warm . . . Only a few feet away from me it's steaming . . .'

Slowly I began to climb the steep slope. I was apprehensive, as if mounting the steps of a magnificent palace to meet a great but terrible personage. Indeed, was this not the abode of the Queen of the Realm of Shades, the impossibly mighty Hel? Primeval thoughts such as these always, in the final assessment, hold greater sway than any amount of scientific objectivity.

'That steam isn't steam at all. It's smoke ... It's getting bloody warm ... The further I go up, the hotter it gets ... At least it's pretty solid under the feet ... I don't fancy falling through a great molten hole ... Ah ... I can smell the sulphur now ... Very strong ...'

I bent to touch a foot-wide pebble, white, heat-split and smoking. It burned my finger-tips. Still the sun burned into my eyes as it had for most of the ascent. If I shielded them I could see but two feet ahead through the smoke. The ground sloped at about forty-five degrees and I had to pick my way through great shapeless rocks five feet, seven feet and more high, strewn carelessly about. The higher I climbed the hotter became the air in my nostrils and lungs. Onward I went; up, up into the sun. There should have been an orchestra somewhere, belting out Wagner. The cinders crunched underfoot as I breathed the sulphurous fumes. Then I was there!

'Here it is!' I shouted with panting breath. 'I'm at the top of Hekla ...! And what a sight ...! There's a great hole here ... It's smoking. There's smoke coming out of it ... Smoke coming from all around ...'

Awesome it was; awesome beyond imagination. The raw power of the earth. This hole, plugged tenuously by a few feet of newly solidified lava, went straight to the earth's core. The enormity of it all seeped into my being and it was impossible not to indulge in formless, pre-adamite, worship.

'Gaze – gaze – O mortal men ... Gaze into the great gaping maw of Hell ...'

I stood on the edge and peered over the rim. The far rim of

the crater was over five hundred feet away and over half a mile from my left to my right. The edges of the great oval hole were uneven in a complete denial of order. I found a fairly level area, perhaps fifteen feet square, upon which to stand. Here the volcano, reaching its optimum height, flattened out briefly before falling into its own centre. Mighty rocks, sharp-edged and intimidating, leaned at unlikely angles amid great piles of smoking cinders.

I looked down through the smoke and steam. The edge lava had collapsed back, plugging the crater and making an un-even funnel of grey-black rock, ash and jagged aa lava slashed by streaks of yellow sulphur and red iron oxide through which seeped the smoke and sulphur fumes in dancing, weaving wraiths. The bottom of the funnel was three hundred feet down through the haze and looked very hot indeed. The whole crater was mesmerising, drawing my entire conscious-ness to it like nothing I had ever experienced before. Emotions of deep awe, shock, exultation, wonder, rapture and fear churned together in an inseparable mêlée.

And the setting for this colossal gateway was no less spec-tacular. To the western horizon and two thousand feet below, a flat, white table-cloth of cloud reflected, in eye-hurting bril-liance, the cold, clean sun. Below the mountain this table-cloth gradually became lace-edged and finally allowed the land to show itself uncovered. Lakes there were, and the Thjórsá river written in silver to the north; whilst to the south, fifty miles distant, the grey North Atlantic suggested its pre-sence beyond subservient tall peaks and glaciers. Nothing visible was higher than was I, but the pride of this was mixed with the humility of my own insignificance amidst such gran-deur. Here was the abode of gods, and I but a visiting mortal.

Standing and staring had to be rationed. Six o'clock was, I decided, departure time. It was fast approaching and there was work to be done. I set up my camera, posed on the edge of the crater, and almost presented posterity with an excellent shot of myself plummeting into Hell as the rim gave way beneath me. I stepped back as cinders cascaded into the depths. Never look askance at the poseur; his way of life is fraught with danger.

A temporary cairn had been erected at the rim's highest point, a monument to the audacity of transient man. Atop this, side by side in majesty, sat two ancient and venerable size nine boots, their days of labour past and conveyed to their reward by a grateful owner. What more fitting end could a pair of loyal boots wish? There was something poetic, and basically just, about those boots poised at the highest visible pinnacle. The lowly had indeed been exalted. Cinderella was indubitably a true story.

As I opened up a film canister to replace the exposed footage a little trickle of yellow sand fell onto the black rim-lava. This was an unused film from my last Sahara trip, so there is now a bit of the Sahara at Hell's gate. I ate some chocolate, and made the mistake of putting the bar down. It melted. My feet were becoming uncomfortably hot despite the thick rubber soles of my boots, though a stiff breeze kept my body cool.

At six I left the summit and turned for the plain. It had taken me almost nine hours to climb the volcano, but I had to reach the plain in much less. The cloud was coming in fast and the sun was dropping from the sky. It was Tungnafellsjökull writ large. Soon I was below the cone and on the first snow-field. I followed my footprints along its edge, very carefully, remembering my near-disaster on the ascent. It was much easier with both the sun and the wind at my back, but the slope was still at forty-five degrees so caution was the rule. I would have given much for the magical appearance of a hang-glider parked on the snow. This activity I had enjoyed for many years, and to sail out over that plain, wheeling and sea-gull dipping, would have been indescribably wonderful.

Reaching the first chaotic vent I decided to avoid it by staying beneath it on the face of the mountain. There was deep tephra, but it was manageable. Soon I gained the next, shallower-sloped snow-field and continued along its upper edge, still following my own footprints. At the end of this field I thought it best to remain on the face rather than be caught amongst the new lava-fields of the ridge. There was more elbow-room on the *outside* of the mountain, and progress was much more discernible. But it was not to be. Very deep tephra made progress much too difficult so I climbed back to the ridge.

On another snow-field I saw my footprints again, and those of my etheric companion both ascending and descending. *Bigfoot* was not far ahead. We must have passed each other as I was still climbing up. Again the layer-cake snow, and again the petrified forest. I received a very bad gash to my right wrist which bled very well, making my hand sticky and leaving brilliant red spots on the snow.

At eight o'clock I was below the snow-line. Progress had been excellent and I was justly pleased as I bounced over the quite hard black surface. At eight-thirty I looked back and Hekla, all but the summit itself, was shrouded in cloud, like pink candy-floss lit by the sinking red sun. I had barely made it in time.

But hurry must be paid for. I had neglected to fill my water-bottle with snow, thinking to do so when I met again the great white wedge of my ascent. Unfortunately, in the twilight, I had missed my morning footprints, and therefore the snow-wedge, and was very thirsty indeed. I found myself amongst another stone forest, older than the others with a sparcity of trees. There was tethra covering the forest floor which placed it as having been laid at the latest in 1980, and possibly much earlier as there were signs of erosion. At nine, with the temperature dropping almost to freezing, I was through it and on the plain. There was a patch of tephra-covered snow on a slope, thin and hard. I was desperately thirsty and, using my keys, chipped out a small pile of grey, frozen mud which I put into my bottle to melt. It looked revolting, but would be sterile and, when the mud sank to the bottom, should be drinkable.

As almost complete darkness descended I found tracks of a vehicle going my way, heading for the road. The only light was from the stars, coldly twinkling in the blackness of space, coloured and incredibly numerous, as above a desert. The pole star was almost at the zenith, and directly above me. My compasses were useless, of course, so navigation was simply by placing myself in relation to Hekla, still glowing faintly in the sunlight. My watch proclaimed ten o'clock. In two hours, it seemed, I should reach base-camp.

I had with me a small torch which was occasionally useful to highlight details, but was mostly ignored in favour of *subliminal sight*, a technique whereby one follows the barely discernible track not by direct, hard looking, but by *half-looking* and letting the brain, of its own accord, decide the subtleties of greyness that denote the previous passage of others.

The tracks were joined by others, and I passed the point where the morning's track joined the one I was now on. I decided to stick with this one as it was more distinct, and according to the map, a more direct route to the road. And that was my third mistake!

At ten-thirty it veered to the right when it encountered a massive new stone forest, its trees stark and menacing against the star-lit sky, towering like a regiment of evil giants. Ten minutes later the track ended in a churning of tyre-marks at the base of a small volcano. I knew that the road must be within a mile of me, beyond that impassable stone barrier. The track had obviously been covered by the 1981 eruption. For a while I tried to find a way around the lava, but gave up when my torch batteries died. Back to the vehicle tracks I went, and tried skirting the lava to the west, going cross-country in hope and moving roughly in the direction of camp. My breath was visible, denoting the freezing temperature. It became more likely that I would have to bivi down for a cold night, but not yet.

There was a great flash across the sky, unexpected, nerve-tingling. I looked up and saw a grey streak of ice-cloud hanging in the sky from horizon to horizon. The western end was caught in the rays of a sun which was below my horizon. Each ice-particle reflected this light to its neighbour, which did the same in a brilliant chain-reaction athwart the heavens. The light flashed and weaved a celestial ballet above me as curtains of light hung in the upper air. The sky was a mass of moving light; even shooting-stars joined the dance and streaked through the light-clouds to blot from my mind all but pure enjoyment.

It was the northern lights, the aurora borealis spoken of by mariners and explorers in tones of rapture. I had never really believed the floweriness of their accounts, putting it down to their desire to impress and entertain; but here it was, displaying for me, a far more wondrous sight than could ever be conveyed by mere words. This was Mystical, the work of gods. I could see the shining armour of the Valkyries and hear the thunder of their horses as they raced through the sky. Had they come for me? I found my hand clutching the handle of My Father's Sword at my hip as I awaited their kiss and hoped against hope that I be deemed worthy. Valhalla and its delights seemed less remote in legend and mightily, mightily sweet.

I lay on my back the better to see the show. For some time I lay and enjoyed the sky, smiling the widest of child-like smiles and repeating to myself, over and over, an involuntary 'Oh . . .! Oh . . .! Oh . . .!'

There was an interval in the show and I realised that I was very cold indeed. Once more I sallied forth in search of my illusive camp. The forest petered out and it was possible, with care, to head directly for the road, keeping the barely visible Hekla at my back. At about twelve-thirty I began to have severe doubts about whether I had inadvertently crossed the road in the dark. A long cerebral debate ensued, but came to no acceptable conclusion. Fatigue was heavy on me and movement was automatic. It was five hours or so to the beginnings of dawn. To wander aimlessly, not being sure of direction, was pointless. I would have to rest up for the night. If I dressed in my wind- and water-proofs then survival was assured. There was a small rocky hill dimly close which promised some shelter from the wind so I went towards it, mentally prepared for a cold and uncomfortable few hours.

There was a short drop; a mere six inches or so, and the ground ceased to crunch underfoot. Three strides further and the land rose to cinders again. Back to the dip I went, and kneeling, felt the invisible ground like a blind man. There were two very hard channels a few feet apart with cinders between. It was the road. I danced a little jig, fatigue forgotten, and the sky joined in with gusto, the aurora borealis flashing outward from the zenith and sending streaks of light to every horizon. Joy upon joy abounded.

West I went, a new spring in my step. At about one-thirty a vehicle came in the opposite direction, lights scything the darkness. I waved happily to the occupants and the driver honked his horn. Then I was alone again with the dark and the light.

At about half-past two I realised that something was wrong. I could see the lights of the hydroelectric plant, and they were only a couple of miles away. My camp was about five miles from those lights. Somehow I had passed it by. Whether I had done so whilst I had been on the road, or whilst searching for it, I did not know; and I was too fatigued to be bothered trying to work it out. I sat for a while on a rock and took a drink of mud, sifting out the tephra with my teeth. A car's headlights raced along a road atop some small hills two miles away. I was amazed at its speed. Then I realised that it was the crescent moon rising; Mani in his silver chariot. It hung static in the sky and there was neither road nor car. My fatigue was such that perception was being affected.

After a rest I wearily retraced my steps to the east, looking for the rock which marked my base-camp. It was four-fifteen when I located the little, incredibly welcome, bivi and crawled into my sleeping-bag. I removed only my boots and noticed a lightening of the sky before I zipped myself into my cocoon and became oblivious of the universe. I had been walking for almost twenty-two-and-a-half hours and was a little weary.

8   Sprengisandur Again

A supermarket is the most wonderful place on earth. It is all one's birthdays rolled together with Christmas on top. I had taken a lift that morning from a tourist coach which dropped me in Hella, a small, neat, modern village/town some thirty miles to the west of my base-camp. After my exertions of the previous day, and indeed the recent fortnight, I considered a decent, restaurant-cooked meal to be in order. For two days I had eaten little but biscuits and stale bread, and the prospect of a real meal from a plate had filled my mind that morning to the point of ecstasy. Before I tackled Sprengisandur again I had to replenish my dwindling food supplies, so to Hella I had to go.

I passed shelves of biscuits brilliant in coloured cellophane, cold vacuum-packed sausages, tins of meat and fish, orange-juice, cheese, chocolate, *fresh* bread and milk. My basket became ominously heavy as, uncontrolled, I grabbed from the shelves and clutched each item gleefully. I had to carefully edit my hoard before approaching the check-out.

Everything was incredibly expensive by British standards, being priced at three, four, and even five times their cost at home. I tried to shut my mind to such things and paid the mighty bill with good grace. Sitting on the porch in the sun, people passing by, I opened a litre carton of milk. The instructions for accomplishing this feat were written in the Lancashire dialect.

'*Opnið hér*', it read, with an arrow pointing to the correct side which bore the legend, '*Rífið upp hér*'. These would be pronounced almost as 'Oppen-it here', and 'Rip it up here', which I thought were the finest and most explicit set of instructions ever devised for such an occasion, and yet more proof of my linguistic heritage.

The cold milk ran down my throat, parched since drinking the mud in the night, and sang throughout my insides, finding crevice after crevice into which to flow, cooling and rejuvenating, bringing life to body and happiness to soul. The carton was empty when I took it from my lips and sighed at the day.

The restaurant was close by, overlooking the main road which here was actually metalled. There were tables and chairs outside beneath an awning, but a cool breeze dictated that I enter the portals. It was neat, spotless and alcoved with pine tables and fringed lights. From a muted radio came the voice of Gracie Fields, or her impersonator, singing an Icelandic song in a Rochdale accent as the few customers chatted over their midday meal. The system was self-service so, dumping my rucksack in the porch, I ordered pork cutlets and chips from the starched chef, ferried a bowl of soup to a table, and tried to make something resembling tea from the hot water and dust-bags provided. The soup was excellent and warming, and the pork cutlets, swimming in mustard sauce with vegetables and *French-fries*, were fit for the tables of kings. There was nothing on the plate but a minute piece of gristle and a smudge of grease when it was borne away. It was necessary to end the meal in style by consuming a large and sticky slice of cream cake and a *beer*.

As I sat contemplating the wonders of the culinary art a bus pulled up outside disgorging a small army of babbling tourists who made a direct frontal assault upon the restaurant. Bursting open the doors and flooding into every cranny of the building bent on the enjoyment of sustenance, they shouted and cajoled, and elbowed and jostled in good-natured rapine. Suddenly two figures emerged from the seething mass of multi-coloured humanity and commenced to shake me gleefully and energetically by the hand. It was Slim and The

Engineer, grinning all over wind-tanned faces and enthusing over this unexpected meeting. As always it was good to see familiar faces in a strange land and we chatted over drinks, the instant party continuing around us.

'We had a ride to Landmannalaugar with some tourists,' said Slim. Landmannalaugar was one of the most beautiful, and therefore the most *touristy*, of the tourist huts, which boasted hot springs to swim in.

'There were many tourists,' confirmed The Engineer. 'They became very drunk and sang all night near the springs.'

'We could not sleep because of the noise,' said Slim, sadly.

'You should have joined them,' I suggested, which seemed like an excellent way to solve the problem.

'They bring their own alcohol,' The Engineer explained. 'We could not buy it in Iceland. It is possible to buy it in Reykjavik, but it is much too expensive.'

'The Icelanders drink alcohol maybe once or twice a year, when there is a wedding, or perhaps at another important time,' said Slim. 'They are not used to it and get drunk very easily.'

The Engineer told the tale of a conference in Germany attended by some Icelanders.

'They fell over very quickly and missed most of the conference,' he chuckled, sipping his non-alcoholic German beer with obvious distaste.

I related my tale of the climbing of Hekla, including the search for my base-camp along the road beneath the northern lights. A look of happy surprise came upon the visage of The Engineer. 'Then you are *The Mad Night Walker*!' he said, as if he were pronouncing the name of some legendary hero.

'Eh?' said I in puzzlement. Slim took over the story.

'Some tourists came to the hut early this morning and told us that when they were driving down the road they saw a walker laughing and waving in the middle of the night like a madman.'

We confirmed the road and I admitted liability. There was comment on the smallness of the planet and we laughed and talked some more.

The sun had been streaming in through the windows making the restaurant's interior bright. Suddenly the brightness diminished and dark corners expanded into the room. There was a rhythmic tremble of the ground and the roar of humanity shrank to a whisper of anticipation. Darkness descended upon the porch like the dropping of night. The door slowly opened inwards and all the restaurant gazed at the stooping, laden figure and mighty, grinning face of Hermann the German.

Good-naturedly he entered, the people making room, and effortlessly removed his rucksack with one hand, placing it beside mine. He smiled a tombstone smile and gazed around the room, the people smiling nervously back. Then he saw me and his face split laterally.

'Ach zo!' he said pleasantly. All the glasses rattled on the shelves. He came towards me, spade-hand outstretched, and the people parted like the Red Sea before Moses. He engulfed my hand warmly in his, and we were happy at the meeting.

'How are joo? How vas ze lava?' He saw my scarred boots. 'It vas hard, ja?' Outside the ladies of Hella looked anxiously at the sky and quickly took in their washing.

'Yes, it was very hard.' I grinned. 'You were right.' We talked of the lava desert, of the flies of Mývatn, and of Sprengisandur. He had travelled to these places by bus, on foot and by hitching lifts. Hermann was enjoying his holiday.

'Yesterday I climbed Hekla,' I told him proudly, preening a little.

'Yesterday?' he gently bellowed. 'I alzo climbed Hekla yesterday!'

Light began to dawn. I took out my map. 'Did you go this way?' I asked, pointing out my route.

'Ja – ja! Und joo alzo?'

'Yes. And you were on top at four o'clock.'

'Jawohl! Zo it vas joor feets I see in der snow on ze vay down!'

Bigfoot was Hermann the German. We laughed uproariously and slapped each other's backs as the tourists retreated en masse towards the supermarket, jamming each other in the doorway.

We talked and laughed together for a while; Slim, Hermann, The Engineer and me. It was the kind of time that needed pints of good ale to mark it in personal histories, but it was not to be. Soon the tourist bus made signs of leaving and Slim and The Engineer went with it, hands waving, towards the waterfall of Gullfoss. Hermann remained a while longer, then loaded up and, mighty hand signing a farewell, walked towards Reykjavik to smell the blood of other Englishmen. There was no longer a reason for my presence in Hella so I settled my rucksack on my shoulders and took the road leading to my appointment with Sprengisandur.

Very quickly I was picked up by a large lorry which decanted me near the hydroelectric plant in the shadow of Hekla. Then it sped down the track that led past my Hekla base-camp leaving me alone beneath the conquered volcano which brooded in defeat. It had occurred to me that I would not require much of my equipment for the second half of Sprengisandur, so the sensible thing to do was to leave it somewhere and pick it up later in passing. There was something about Icelanders that exuded honesty and I had no worries about leaving things in custody. I had spoken with the dam-workers prior to my ascent of Hekla and thought that they might be willing to look after the heaviest items for me. They were there on the dam, two men and a boy. Yes, they said, they would keep an eye on it for a few days. I left all my camera and climbing equipment with them, and various other items, thus reducing my load to little over twenty pounds. I thanked them and continued up the Sprengisandur road towards the hut.

A big cross-country estate car crunched to a halt. Down came the window and a big red face stuck out. It had a fat neck beneath and an enormous arm clad in red woollen tartan. Happy eyes twinkled between crow's-feet and half a huge cigar poked from the side of a toothy, grinning mouth.

'How fur ya goin' feller?' he asked in an accent I had heard only in John Wayne movies.

' 'Bout a hunderd miles,' I said, dropping automatically into transatlantic, or at least making the attempt. I have found from experience that no American can understand a word of Lancastrian.

'Reckon ah kin do thet. Come aboard,' he said with jollity. He was alone so I climbed into the right-hand seat and off we went east, the big tyres eating up the miles. Big and round he was, his short cropped hair an iron grey. Had he a long white beard he would have looked fine in charge of reindeer.

'Ma name's Hank,' he said. 'Got a li'l spread out west. Like t' come ta Ice-land 'cause this is where ma folks came from, way back.' An American rancher named Hank – the whole thing had a certain surreal aspect. I introduced myself and told him I was wandering around Iceland; the details of why I was heading into Sprengisandur in order to walk out again I considered too complicated to inflict upon my unsuspecting benefactor.

Hank knew about Iceland, and gave me a running commentary of his personal view of it. The three hours or so I spent with him opened up for me the annals, the Sagas, and the whole feel of the land. He spoke casually, thinking of each word before letting it issue forth, and laying it before me like a present to be enjoyed. He was an entertainer, and a purveyor of trinkets. I liked Hank very much.

The car entered the southern barren reaches of Sprengisandur. 'Coupla hunderd years ago,' said Hank, 'was a outlaw lived 'round here. Name of Eyvind; Eyvind of the Mountains. Pretty tough kinda feller. Went around robbin' an' thievin' an' all. Guess folks didn't like him a whole lot so they chased him out to the desert. Lived out in Sprengisandur fer years. Had him a wife too. Name of Halla. Folks said he could make almost anythin' outa nothin'. He made baskets outa twigs. Made 'em so fine you could carry water in 'em. Imagine that! A basket fulla water. Didn't leak none neither. Weird guy, this Eyvind. Said he could move faster'n a horse by doin' cart-wheels. Called it *hand-runnin'*! Takes all kinds. Why'd he wanna do that I wonder? They was outlaws fer more'n twenty years, then they got 'em a pardon and went back home.'

I imagined Eyvind the robber living in that desolate land, shunned by his kind, surviving on little but the proceeds of his villainy, yet such a craftsman as to be capable of honest greatness. Strange are the workings of the human mind.

'There's all kinda things named after Eyvind; rivers, an' a bog, an' up near Mývatn when they get a thick mist they call it Eyvind's-mist 'cause he escaped into the mist once. How does a guy like that git things named after him?'

There was a deep ford which the car took in its stride, but would have given trouble to a lesser vehicle. 'Used to be a bridge here. Got washed away by the floods. It's a dangerous place. Folks git killed here sometimes. You gotta watch what you're doin' here. Ain't no place to fool around.' I made note of the warning for my return journey.

The road was no longer metalled, but was of good quality and had obviously been recently worked on. I mentioned this to Hank.

'Yea, there's a whole lotta hydroelectric schemes goin' on around here. A whole heapa buildin' an' diggin' an' shiftin'. The old road weren't good enough fer the trucks and the earth-movers so they rebuilt it. It shore is better. These folks here are real workers. Maybe if they git the electricity they can git some sorta industry goin'. There ain't no iron here, so they'd have to import that. They got nothin' but fish. Around eighty per cent of their export earnings is from fish, an' that ain't gonna last much longer. Most fish only git chance to spawn once in their lifetime. It ain't enough to keep the stocks up. They spawn, and then they git caught. Real soon there ain't gonna be no fish left at all.'

We bounced on down the new road, past construction work and heavy plant as Iceland fought to keep its place in the twentieth century. Soon we were on unmade road again, driving through the softly rolling black desert. The sky was clouding over and Hofsjökull was a mighty white streak to the left, dominating the vista. There was greenery at its feet, amid the brilliant streaks of water.

Hank's powerful hands eagerly clutched the bucking wheel. 'Know much about the history of Ice-land?' he asked, seeking for a cue. I knew the outline but I wanted to hear Hank tell it.

'Nope,' I said. 'Not a lot.' Hank was happy at this, took a puff at his new cigar and filled his lungs with the smoke.

Then he told of how Naddod and Gardar Svavarsson found the land by accident, of how Raven Floki stayed awhile, of Ingolf who founded Reykjavik and of how the other refugees from the fierce hand of Harald Fine-hair colonised the land.

'Pretty soon,' said Hank, 'there was a land-rush. Folks came from all over. Most came from Norway to git away from Harald Ass-hole, but they came from the Faroes, the Shitlands, Britain and Ire-land too. These guys were ruled by a bunch of fellers called the *goðar*, that's plural fer *goði*. A goði was a sorta mixture of priest and lord, and he'd be the king-pin of his district. He was elected by common consent. 'Course it was easier to git elected if ya had more soldiers than the next guy. It was his job to supply oxen or horses fer sacrifice, 'cause they was pagans. Most of 'em worshipped Thor, bein' warriors an' all, but some figured they'd be better off with Oðin bein' as how he was chief god.

'Well, around the beginnin' of the tenth century they sorta figured they'd have themselves a nation instead of a lotta little warlords a-bickerin' amongst 'emselves, so the goðar sent a real smart feller called Ulfljót to Norway to sort out a set of laws to live by. He adapted the laws of Norway to the needs of Ice-land and in 930 came back to tell the folks here-abouts.

'The goðar and the free-men all gathered on a plain near a lake in west Ice-land, biggest lake in the whole goddam island, and held a *Althing*, that's what they called their gennal-assembly. Called the lake *Thingvallavatn*. Now this Ufljót was the only guy that knew the law so they elected him as *Lawspeaker*. The Lawspeaker held his job fer three years and then they had elections. He recited a third of the law every year from the top of a rock called the Law Rock. This guy didn't have no power 'cause the goðar had all-a that, but he sure as Hell had a lotta influence. I guess the government was pretty right-wing an' all. Like I said, they was pagans, so they had pagan laws. Had one law that ships at sea shouldn't have figure-heads, an' if they did then they had ta take 'em off afore they sighted land in case the gapin' dragon-heads upset the local spirits. These guys didn't take no chances.

'After 930 Christianity started ta move in. It had taken over in Europe, Scandinavia and the British Isles, but Ice-land held out until AD 1000 when it was officially adopted at the *Althing* to prevent civil war. This helped tradin' with other countries a whole heap. Was a guy called Erik the Red sailed out west. Discovered Green-land. It weren't too green but he figured a nice name wouldn't do it no harm. His son, Leif Eriksson, sailed further west and discovered America around Labrador near five hundred years afore Columbus was born. Called it

Vin-land on account there was grape-vines a-growin'. Musta been a mite warmer in those days.

'Well, things weren't too good back home, with little wars goin' on 'mongst the goðar. The kings o' Norway was hoverin' like vultures an' in 1264 the Norwegians took over to *protect* 'em. Come the fourteenth century they found 'emselves under Denmark in a union with Norway and Sweden and that's the way things were fer six hunderd years. Had the same problems as all-a Europe, what with the Black Death, the Reformation an' all. Around the sixteenth and seventeenth centuries there was a lotta volcanoes goin' off all over, spreadin' ash on good farmland and a whole bunch o' folks starved ta death.

'Around the end of the nineteenth century Denmark was bein' a real pain with a passel of trade monopolies so the folks started a-gettin' the old nationalist feelin' again. Got 'em partial home rule in 1904 and come 1918 they'd independence under the Danish crown. Then in 1940 Ay-dolf Hitler took a likin' ta Danish pastry so he invaded Denmark. Now Ice-land would-a been a real handy base in the North Atlantic fer old Ay-dolf's navy an' air-force, an' it didn't have much of a de-fence force, so the British came in to keep him out. Next year the Yew-essuv-ay took over from the British an' even built a airfield at Keflavik to help trans-atlantic communications. Come 1944, after nigh-on seven hunderd years of foreign rule, they became a republic and got their full independence agin.'

I caught a glimpse of red ahead; the roof of the hut about a half-mile away. I didn't want to go to it as this would mean saying hello to Val and Brynhild, relating recent events and inevitably spending the night there. It was early evening with a few hours of walking left in the day, and time was getting short.

'Can you drop me here, Hank?' I requested.

'Shore. Hut's just ahead. I'll drop you there.'

'Right here's fine. I wanna camp near the river,' I lied.

'Fine. If that's what ya want,' he grinned, reining in the car. I'll swear he said, 'Woa!'

I thanked him for the ride and shook his hand.

'Take care now, ya hear? Look out fer that Eyvind. They say his ghost still haunts these here parts.' We both laughed, easily. 'So-long feller.'

'So long, Hank. Have a good trip.' With a wave he was gone, his engine noise fading into nothing.

Hofsjökul's low, white dome gleamed to the west eleven miles away, cold and silent. Upper tributaries of the Thjórsá separated me from it. For the next few days I would never be far from the route of Kristinn the shepherd, in very similar conditions to those he experienced, for the days of sun were over. I thanked providence that I was better equipped than he, picked up my much lighter rucksack and turned south-west, the glacier glistening Christmas-like to my right and the black rolling sand-dunes of Sprengisandur going on forever.

For three hours I walked back along the track, the sky clouding rapidly but the wind, thankfully, remaining gentle. It became dark, a dismal, starless dark. I found a place away from the track and set up camp. It began to rain. I have this effect upon deserts.

The rain was heavy and steady, battering my ears as I lay in my bivi. I noticed that I had a fever, my limbs shivering uncontrollably. Everything ached and sharp pains shot without warning through my feet, the nerves seemingly short-circuiting. The previous day my body had received a battering such as no body should have to take, and now had come the reckoning. The pained members had a word with the shop-steward, the brain.

'Why are we being battered thus?' they wished to know. The shop-steward had words with Head Office, the mind.

'Look, lads,' said the chairman of the board, 'we've got to

get this job finished on time. I'm sorry but you'll have to put up with it for a while longer. When we've done you can have a *good* rest.' Then he smiled, and went back to his thinking. The members mumbled and muttered, but dispersed, each dwelling upon his private ills.

I knew that I had damaged myself quite severely, but equally well I knew that the only way to keep the pain at bay was to keep walking, to breach the pain-barrier by throwing such a quantity of pain at the brain that it simply couldn't handle it and gave up trying. It was a technique I had used often. Not a pleasant method, but it worked. In order to achieve what I had set out to achieve there was no alternative. These thoughts were on my mind as I drifted away from the mundane world into limbo.

It rained all the seventeenth day, and the wind blew. From time to time the low cloud would lift a little from Hofsjökull to my right, but as the day dragged on the glacier fell behind me and was forgotten. The day was like a penance for all the evils I had perpetrated throughout life. It seemed a suitable punishment for muggers. I pictured the judge, black cap upon his wig, pronouncing in sepulchral tones, 'I sentence you to walk Sprengisandur . . . and may God have mercy upon your soul!' The look of horror upon the face of the thug. The letters to *The Times* containing words like *barbaric* and *inhuman*. It would not be a short sharp shock, but a long dull one, and the mugger, I guarantee, would never mug again.

> *Sprengisandur – Sprengisandur.*
> *Bloody great draining-board, Sprengisandur . . .*

That day I covered thirty miles. I camped near a bridge over a ravine, and slept with the roar of the waters in my ears.

*　　　*　　　*

It was still raining the next day. I was fed-up . . . with the wind, with the rain, but mostly with Sprengisandur! When I am fed-up I write songs, usually about being fed-up. As I walked down the interminable track I juggled notes and metaphors, and began to think of the song-writers and poets of Iceland. Theirs is a fine tradition stretching back to their Norwegian origins over a thousand years ago. This tradition rests on three pillars, Skaldic poetry, the Sagas and the Eddas. The first are poems written to rigid rules of metre, accentuation, alliteration and rhyme into which are intricately woven euphemisms and metaphors. The result is a kind of cross between a zen coan and a limerick. The Sagas, conversely, are tales of blood and thunder, of gods, of heroes and of battles. It is the content, rather than the presentation, that is important. The tales are long and, though based upon facts of national or family history, owe much to poetic licence to improve the story.

The Eddas are not entities in themselves, but more like magazines, or anthologies of history, poetry, myths, proverbs and even statements of the complex rules of poetry itself. At the beginning of the thirteenth century the acknowledged master, Snorri Sturluson, wrote the most memorable contributions to the genre. But Icelandic literature was not my concern as I plodded Sprengisandur that cold, wet, gusty day. Only escape was on my mind as I rearranged words and notes to some semblance of order.

> *Sprengisandur – Sprengisandur . . .*
> *Uninspirational – Sprengisandur . . .*

I arrived at the dangerous ford of which Hank the Yank had warned me. It looked forbidding, the grey-brown waters of indeterminate depth. As I stood contemplating my next move a Land Rover came along the track in my direction. He was full, but allowed me to cling to the back, spider-like, as he traversed the swirling torrent. It was worrying as the vehicle bucked and bounced through the rush of the waters for to fall would have given Old Baldie the victory he so diligently sought. Beyond the river, wet from the spray, I continued walking towards Hekla, now invisible somewhere in the low cloud. When I had walked thirty-two miles I stopped walking, and camped, and slept.

The next morning I was only two hours' walk from the hydro-scheme. The workmen didn't seem to have moved during the intervening three days. I sadly piled all my other gear onto my back, thanked them, and continued to do what walking machines do, in the rain. I had crossed the river at the dam and was now heading west alongside its meandering towards a road junction that would take me north to Gullfoss, the 'Golden Waterfall', which was my next destination, and which I expected to encounter in about two days. The land was now pastoral with barbed-wire fences, sheep and Icelandic ponies, short and stocky with flowing manes now hanging wetly on powerful necks. Burfell, shrouded and damply unseen, was to my left and I must have passed within a mile of where the gallant Kristinn was discovered. In the evening I found my junction, turned right, crossed a very long bridge and camped beyond it on *grass*.

It was the following evening, after another day of the same, when a car pulled up in the rain. The driver bravely wound down his window and spoke through the wind and water.

'Where do you go?'

'To Gullfoss.'

'I have a farm near Gullfoss. You can sleep in my hay-house,' he said. I thanked him, smiling, and leaped into the warm, dry car. It was the best offer I could hope for, and it got me out of the lashing rain. After four days of the wet my spirits were none too high and inevitably my sleeping-bag had become wet. The prospect of a dry barn was a wonderful thing.

'I am Maggnús Grimsson,' he said. Always in Iceland a person is introduced by his full name. I introduced myself, stating my origins.

'You will be dry in my hay-house,' he said, pleasantly. 'Is that right, *hay-house*?'

'We usually say *barn* or *hay-loft*, but *hay-house* is fine,' I explained, smiling all over my wet face.

'*Barn . . . hay-loft*,' he said, trying the words for size. He filed them away and nodded at his new acquisitions. I judged him to be in his early forties, greying a little and with the lean strength of one used to labour. I never saw him smile, but there was about him a deep contentedness that needed no smile to mark moments of happiness. His life was his farm and his family, a solid stand-point from which he communicated with the world.

The car turned almost immediately up a side-track to the right and crossed a bridge over a full and turgid river.

'Gullfoss is on my land,' he said proudly. 'Tomorrow you can see it from this side. All the tourists see it from the other side.' He spoke English well, but with the hesitancy of one unaccustomed in its use. Sometimes he would speak a word questioningly, seeking confirmation as to its correct usage like the man of precision that he was. 'You can eat with us tonight. My wife will make a good meal.' The prospect of a cooked meal was wonderful for it was four days since my last. I thanked Maggnús profusely and drooled quietly as the car neared a collection of new buildings along a straight dirt road. There was more than one farm here, banding together to form a community.

The hay-house was wonderfully dry, built of breeze-blocks with a corrugated metal roof. I spread out my sleeping-bag to dry and was descended upon by several small children, genderless and warmly wrapped, who required to be thrown around the hay by their new-found playmate amidst the happy bouncing of a couple of friendly, tail-wagging sheep-dogs. Maggnús introduced his wife, a pretty blonde lady, and his eldest son, a young man in his late teens. They were in the milking parlour, attaching the milking machine to the teats of very small cows which came barely to my chest. I watched the operation with interest.

'These are not so big as English cows,' said Maggnús, 'but they are good for milking. I have seen your Jersey cows. They are very big.' I admitted this. He told me the yield of his own cows, with pride, and asked me what the yield of a Jersey would be.

'I have no idea at all,' I admitted.

'Ah,' said his wife, smiling sympathetically, 'you are a city boy.'

I smiled, with perhaps a little sadness. My understanding of the ways of agriculture and animal husbandry was very basic indeed, lamentably so for one who loves the ways of a nature which must cohabit with both these activities. For most of my life I had harboured a wish that someday I would inhabit a standard English cottage adjacent to hills, there to enjoy the tranquillity of the countryside unto dotage. It had been shocking to be confronted, one day of cogitation, with the realisation that all the things I held dear – the variety of conversation, the spectrum of opinion, the availability of knowledge and the infinite diversity of humanity – were to be had only within easy reach of a city. Couple this with easy access to the foods and goods of cosmopolis then *townie* I was, and *townie* would remain. The country was, for me, a place to visit, respect and enjoy, but *not* to inhabit.

The children showed me angora rabbits and a plethora of kittens which bridged the gap 'twixt country and town. I knew about kittens and tickled them happily whilst they played 'rip-the-hand'.

They fed me royally in their beautiful modern home, new with all mod-con. There was salt-fish and potatoes with a fish sauce and butter, followed strangely by soup. Then warm and dry the city boy went to sleep amongst crackling, wholesome-smelling hay.

9   Gullfoss, Geysir and Government

Spray hung in the air about a mile away; two great plumes of white water-vapour marking the place of Gullfoss, generally acknowledged to be the most beautiful and awe-inspiring waterfall in Iceland. I was anxious to make its acquaintance. To my left, almost three hundred feet down a great clean-cut fault-gorge, the Hvíta river was swollen by the floodwaters of the past days' rains, and it mashed and mingled like boiling soup. The two miles from the farm had taken two hours, through clinging thickets and bogs, traversing valleys and hills, over broken volcanic boulders and along narrow sheep-tracks. My rucksack and equipment I had left at the barn since I must return there. In my hand was my cine-camera wrapped in a plastic supermarket bag against the morning drizzle.

The waters below sent up sounds of dissent, but these were muted as I moved from the edge to find an easier route. Silently the splay-plumes beckoned, and I heeded their call. Half a mile, and half an hour later, still the waterfall was unseen and unheard. I dropped down a steep slope, scrambling through loose rocks and guarding the precious camera from hurt. A quarter of a mile further the spray hung above me, and still neither sight nor sound. A small plain ended abruptly ahead and the mist arose in a constant curtain from beyond its edge. In reverence I approached the curtain, feeling a tremble of the ground as I neared the drop.

Suddenly my ears were assaulted by an enormous roar of power and Gullfoss displayed herself like a conquered lover. Ahead and below was a great long hole in the earth bottomed by churning grey waters. Three hundred feet wide was the hole, and two hundred deep; and into it, to my right, fell an implausible amount of water. Slowly it fell, sedate as a ballet, reluctant to reach the bottom, enjoying its unrestricted flight. Above it was a flat table-top of deeply turbulent water agitated by yet more falling water as another waterfall fed the lower one in a great rush of magnificence. This fall, at an elbow-bend in the river, was angled across the flow so that the drop was almost a quarter of a mile long and sixty feet or so in depth. The second spray-plume rose from the right-hand end of this great water-curtain as the falling river hit the rocks below.

Suddenly the sun broke through the morning clouds and lit the show like a spotlight. The waters shone in brilliance as Mother Frigga herself appeared, clad in a gown of golden satin decorated with lace of white foam, and within the spray double rainbows shimmered in almost complete circles for her diadems of deity. I knew that the reality of what I saw was simply millions of gallons of murky water falling over hard basalt shelves and rushing to the sea, but it was almost impossible to view it as such. The goddess smiled graciously at my mortal limitations as I paid my humble respects and reflected upon the true reality of what I deigned to call *real*.

Beyond the falls was a level area scarred by vehicle tracks which was inaccessible to me. As I watched a coach bumped and swayed into view and stopped to disgorge multi-hued humanity. They spread like bluebottles over the rocks, waving cameras and shouting irreverently. Their view, though magnificent, could not compare with my own for I could see the whole sweep of the falls whereas they, from their safe and easily attained perch, could see only the end view. It was justly so.

There was filming to be done, with care, for here the rocks were still loose and uninspected for safety. To the right, where the second plume arose, was a rock shelf overlooking the sheer drop to the water-battered rocks beneath. That would be a place from which to film magnificence. I walked over towards it, the rainbows shimmering in the spray, and reached a point of the bank above the first fall. The river was a quarter-mile or so wide here, running gentle and wind-rippled, seemingly unaware of its fate as it approached the great drop. Here the bank was steep and loose with sharp rocks embedded in wet slag and soil. I reached the edge of the waters, lapping nonchalantly at the spray-wet stones. There was an uneven way, perhaps a couple of feet wide, leading left towards where I wished to be. Very carefully I picked my way over the slippery rocks. The sloping bank became a cliff, then an overhang of solid rock, wet and dripping from hanging grasses and lichens. The spray drenched my waterproofs and ran in streams from nose and finger-tips, and the roar of the falls permeated all.

I was as far as I could go, a spit away from where the river switched from the horizontal to the vertical. To slip was to die, to be swept irrevocably over the edge, to be dashed to pulp on the rocks sixty feet below. I was almost totally blinded by the spray on my spectacles. Very carefully I placed my plastic-clad cine-camera on the ledge and leaned my back on the dripping, overhanging rock as I searched my pocket for a handkerchief. Finding it I removed my spectacles and commenced to clean them. All vision gone, save of a swirling amorphous whiteness, my only contacts with the world were the slippery rock-shelf at my feet, the solid wall at my back, the cold spray lashing my face and the tremendous roar of the waters. I noticed a sound even louder than that of the waters and realised that it was the rhythmic pounding of blood in my ears as my heart pumped madly against the fear.

I replaced my specs and saw the enormously powerful vision of the falling waters. Yes, this had to be captured on film. Again vision was blotted out, and again the wiping, this time with the fingers. Quickly I took the pre-set and wound camera from the plastic bag, pointed it at the upper river, pressed the trigger and panned towards the wondrous sight hoping that it would film the scene before its lens was swamped by spray.

Eighteen seconds of whirring and the clockwork motor stopped. It was done. For better or worse I couldn't afford more film for it. As it turned out, it happened to be one of the best shots of the entire trip. I put the now dripping camera back in the bag and, using my fingers as windscreen-wipers, turned for home. As I turned I felt my feet move sideways and instinctively leaped for the next slab of rock. Looking quickly back I saw a thin sliver of stone, which still held the slightly drier shape of my boots where for minutes I had stood, separate itself from the underlying rock and slip gently into the water to be roughly grabbed by the quickening flow and flung unceremoniously into space.

'Why do you do it, Edwards?' I yelled to myself through the roaring tumult.

'Because it's there!' I replied in a ridiculous falsetto.

The enormous feeling of relief which wafted over me was the measure of my tension on the ledge. I grinned from ear to happy ear as I reached the bank's slope and scrambled upwards.

After a while of worship I left the golden waterfall; left her to the tourists dotted confetti-like on the far side, their totally innocent presence seeming somehow sacrilegious.

My next objective was Geysir, the great spout of boiling water that has given the name *geyser* to every other one throughout the world; the Daddy of 'em all. If I could cross Gullfoss to the tourist side it would be a mere five miles away, but I had to go ten miles, back-tracking through the farm to the bridge which I had crossed with Maggnús by car the previous evening. It was early in the drizzly afternoon when I picked up my load from the barn and looked for Maggnús to say my goodbyes. Maggnús was doing arcane things to his tractor when I found him, surrounded by bouncing offspring and happily barking dogs. He wiped his hands on a cloth as I thanked him for his hospitality. 'There is nothing to thank me for,' he said with the true beneficence of the country-bred. I shook his solid hand, we wished each other well and I walked off down the dirt track leaving the little cluster of farm buildings behind.

The rain fell in earnest as I crossed the high narrow bridge and continued along the road from which Maggnús had rescued me. I was passed by half a dozen thin wet children riding fat wet ponies, wet woolly bobbles bobbing on wet woolly hats. They waved cheerfully and trotted off ahead, happy in the knowledge that skin, at least, was fairly waterproof.

At about two miles from Geysir the rain stopped for the day and a little blue sky appeared. Geysir was visible over the intervening fields. Small clouds of steam arose from an area about two hundred yards across and a few low buildings dotted the vicinity. Occasionally a great spurt of brilliant white steam shot silent and true over a hundred feet into the air and hung for a while until it dispersed into nothing. From where I stood it had the aspect of a wild-west ranch after the departure of the Apache.

Within the hour, weary from the road, I arrived at the place. First a couple of tents full of young Germans, cooking pans clanging amongst the banter. A tatty-looking building proclaimed itself to be a hotel. It seemed deserted and derelict, and a tiled pool steamed gently behind it. The air was acrid with sulphur and the whole place had an air of desertion, like a party where nobody came. A metal fence surrounded the area of principal thermal activity to my right and steam arose from various points. There was a short 'Shush!' sound as a great white pencil of steam towered above me and began to drift apart. But that was for later viewing. I was hungry

and willing to part with a fortune for a good meal at a restaurant.

The 'restaurant' turned out to be a hot-dog bar with post-
cards, woolly hats and tourist junk. I ordered two hot-dogs
and a coffee from the two pretty and friendly girls, and chatted
about Geysir to the one who spoke the best English. She was
in the full bloom of youth and acne, a very comely wench soon
to be beautiful. The steam jetted into the air again, silently
beyond the large window and drowned by American pop
'music'.

'How often does Geysir blow?' I asked with the innocence of
the ignorant.

'That one goes every ten minutes,' said the girl with the joy
of the teacher, 'but that is the small Geysir, Strokkur. The big
one, the Great Geysir, is dead.' She smiled ruefully.

It was as if I had been told of the death of a friend of long
ago. 'Dead?' I said, knowing it to be true.

'Yes. For many years now. Maybe it is the stones that
tourists throw in. Maybe it is just too old.' She, who had
youth, spoke the word *old* as if it were the name of some
awesome land of legend, little understood but some day to be
visited. 'Twice in a month the keeper of the Geysir will throw
in soap powder to make it erupt for the *tourists*.' She was
genuinely sad to be the bearer of these tidings and I admit to a
little pride at her not including me in her defamatory enuncia-
tion of *tourists*.

The sun shone theatrically on the white fence. It was time to
use the camera. I crossed the road and entered the deserted
enclosure through a creaking gate beyond which rows of
white stones lay to designate where thou shalt, or thou shalt
not, walk. A notice in English proclaimed that it was dangerous to leave the pathway. Steam escaped from the depths of
Hell from all kinds of cracks and holes; even in the middle of
the path a little wisp arose apologetically. Small pools of
steaming water a foot or two across bubbled and seethed

and murmured, 'Bubble-ubble-splash-plash-plosh-plopple-bubbubble.' I tried to imagine the complexities of the water channels beneath the surface. How deep? Where was the heat-source? I gave up and settled for an enjoyment of the surface manifestations.

At the end of an avenue of white stones, roped off and raised like a catafalque, the mighty Geysir lay in state. A great circle of grey-white lime-stone-like substance, known as *sinter*, surrounded the vent, raised in a mound some five feet or so above the land; and from the vent gentle steam arose like the wraith of the dead legend. As I stood in homage there was a gentle rumble of the ground and a little boiling water breached the rim of the vent to subside immediately in silence, the last death-rattle of a once-great king. Two coaches had arrived at the hot-dog bar and tourists spread throughout the thermal area, laughing and shouting and taking snapshots with expensive cameras; but when they approached Geysir they became reverent and spoke in whispers, as befitted mourners. Twice a month, the girl had said, they poured soap powder into the vent to make it erupt, but that was merely a life-support system. The soul had departed. The king was dead.

Long live the king! Two hundred yards from the deceased, the mini-Geysir Strokkur erupted into the unsullied blue sky leaving a white cloud to challenge its virginity. Many have been the explanations of the geyser phenomenon. One of the most widely accepted was theorised by no less a personage than Robert William Bunsen, he of the science-lab gas burner. According to Bunsen a geyser vent is in the shape of a narrow inverted funnel. This is filled with water and heated from below by volcanic activity. Because of the narrowness of the pipe convection currents are restricted so that the water is hottest at the bottom. Pressure also increases with depth because of the weight of the column of water. The boiling-point, which is dependent upon pressure, also increases with depth.

Therefore, when the water has almost reached boiling-point throughout the column a quick reduction in pressure will set off a violent chain-reaction when localised boiling will relieve pressure causing further boiling. Then the whole contents of the cavity, unable to be contained by it, shoot dramatically through the only avenue of escape – the narrow vent. Got that?

I stood fifteen feet from the hole. Around it was a basin of the grey-white sinter perhaps thirty feet across. As I watched, steam curled up from the hole, itself a couple of feet wide. Others stood about and the atmosphere was one of expectancy. Cameras were at the ready and pointed at the hole. Water, green and clear, overflowed copiously from the hole to fill the bowl, then began to pour back like bath-water down a plug-hole. The people clucked and fluffed like hens. Twice more the bowl filled, and emptied, and the tension mounted. Then, quickly, very quickly, a great green dome of water expanded over the hole, seething whitely at its centre, and exploded upwards with a 'SHUSH!!' of sheer power to a hundred and fifty feet. The whole show had taken a small fraction of a second and shouts of transatlantic delight and frustration permeated the air.

'Did you get it?'

'Gee!'

'Think I missed it that time.'

'Hell!'

'Lookit that.'

'Holy shee-it!'

Then the aftermath. Hot water fell all around me and sulphurous steam swirled madly about. This was a new experience of the power of nature and I revelled in it, a pagan at prayer.

Several times I watched the geyser blow, fascinated by the spectacle. After one of the eruptions I noticed that I was alone. At some stage the coaches had departed and I had been too engrossed to notice their passing. I filmed, and recorded sounds on tape, and when I was full I went once more to the hot-dog bar to smile at the girls.

It was early evening and the road awaited. I had no reason to remain in Geysir so I gorged myself on further hot-dogs, purchased biscuits and chocolate and, bidding the ladies of Geysir a fond farewell, sallied forth once more in the direction of Reykjavik.

I awoke ten miles from Geysir on the morning of my twenty-second day afoot. The sky was sparsely clouded and there was a slight breeze to freshen the skin. Belly full of water and biscuits, I continued down the twin-rutted road, happy in the morning. The previous day I had come little over twenty miles and was now well rested. There was no pressure of time or distance to weigh upon me as I had a mere fifty miles of strolling to go and four days in which to do it.

Steep hills rose to my right and when the sun shone it shone at my back. By lunch-time I was entering the small town of Laugarvatn sitting by a picturesque lake of the same name. The population had been multiplied several-fold by a large camping and caravan site festooned with washing and children. Enquiries dashed my omnipresent hopes of a restaurant meal, the tourist season having officially ended the previous week. Being saturated with hot-dogs I invested in a cheese and ham toastie, a couple of 'beers' and another cheese and ham toastie, all taken leisurely with a conscious wasting of time. Still my mind, conditioned by the previous weeks, needled me with an insistent 'Go-on . . . get up . . . go-go-go-go-on!' but I smilingly ignored it as I sat outside the little hot-dog bar and perused several waves of teenagers entering and leaving.

They seemed innocent, these Icelandic teenagers, unlike the ones at home. They smiled unwary smiles and even their lechery was honest lechery. The milk-drinking boys wore macho studded leather and the girls in mini-skirts sucked cola through straws. They seemed much happier and more contented of eye than their British counterparts. The harsh realities of aimless and lethargic teenage life in western society did not seem to have touched them. Had they jobs? Did they feel that they had worth? I never discovered these things, but they seemed to me like exotic blooms kept beautiful in conservatory isolation. I wished that their conservatory could be strengthened, but was saddened by the thought that some day the glass might break and, as always happens, the beauty be destroyed, leaving room for the hardier weeds. But perhaps I was underestimating their potential and equating beauty with weakness. I hoped so.

On the way out of town I passed a huge educational building on the lake shore. A large green sign saying 'EDDA' was being taken down. 'EDDA' denoted that the building had been used as hostel accommodation for tourists during the summer holidays, another example of the resourcefulness of Iceland. Always this island people has possessed this quality. Had it not been so then they would have left long ago instead of building a free society against all the odds of man and of nature. My next port of call was Thingvallavatn, the lake on the shores of which was held the first free parliament in the world, the Althing, where no king presided over free men. Ten miles away it was, and a good place to stay for that night.

The walk was pleasant, the first five miles being through waving meadow-grass with hills to the right and an extensive plain to the left. Then there was a steep upslope of the road for half a mile and I stood, puffing and panting, at the edge of an aa lava field, old and green with moss. And beyond, five miles distant, sat the huge mirror of Thingvallavatn with hills behind and a geyser spurting some ten miles away on its far shore.

On down the road I passed a car with windows and doors

wide open, its people spread about gathering black berries. From it, ridiculously loud, came the sound of four Liverpudlians belting out '. . . day tripper! Sunday driver – yea!' The trippers waved happily at me, pleased that they had given me this somewhat dubious present of sound. I smiled back, sadly, telling myself to live-and-let-live. 'Try to see it my way . . .,' sang the oblivious quartet, 'We can work it out . . . We can work it out.' Life is, indeed, very short, and there's no ta-ha-ha-ha-haam for fussin' an' fightin' ma friends. Philosophically I walked on towards the distant lake.

It was evening when I set up camp on the lake shore. Ranks of notices forbade fishing during the spawning and everywhere was the evidence of tourism for this area was a park, a national shrine and a place of great beauty. And the people respected it as such for nowhere was there litter or signs of vandalism. Dwarf birch covered the area and I built a fire from their dead wood to make an evening cuppa. Never could the lake have been more beautiful than it was that evening. Glass-like, with just an occasional ripple, it reflected the golden clouds of sunset. Small islands dotted the lake darkly and beyond it there was a cleft in the hills through which, on the morrow, I would go. From there, if the weather were clear, I should be able to see Reykjavik and the sea. The adventure was coming to a close, the hardships behind and the battle won. It is always a sad time, the end of a journey, for it denotes the end of what has been a small, separate life; remote from normal existence and an entity of itself. The desires and aspirations within that small life are very similar to those of the greater journey of life, but because of its short duration they must be more immediate of attainment. There are the minor goals within the greater picture, goals such as the lava desert, the glacier, Sprengisandur and Hekla; but always there is the greater goal, the arrival at the destination, the end of the journey and the end of the life. And with the end of any life comes a gladness for the ending of toil and strain, but also a sadness for the ending of the joys, the jewels in the sea of hurt. I thought of these things as my cup of tea warmed my hands, as the fire gently glowed, and as the sun died behind the hills of Thingvallavatn.

In the high summer of the year the Christians would have called AD 930 a goði whose name, perhaps, was Olaf rode his pony up the steep track towards the great lake. With him, one upon either side, rode men of dignity, iron-bladed swords slapping their thighs and the wind in their faces disturbing good blond beards. The beard of the goði contained the hard grey hair of wisdom and his eyes were deep and searching of gaze. Behind, snaking for further than a man could throw, came men and women leading pack-horses laden with pots and pans of iron, woven woollen cloth, dried fish, ornaments and all manner of goods for trade.

They topped the rise and stopped. The lake lay flat and shining with mountains about, and at its northern shore a great mass of people, tents, animals; and even at this distance they could hear the hum and rattle of population. It was a new thing for Iceland, the first gathering of the people for the hearing of laws and the holding of courts, and the smile on the weathered face of the goði said that it was good. He dug his heels into his mount and they continued through the ancient columns of lava, covered greenly by lichen and moss, as the women darted here and there picking the early black berries.

On the shores of the lake they set their camp for two weeks of living and the goði searched the other camps for old friends, and for news. Men fished the lake-waters hauling in nets heavy with trout, and goods of all kinds were sold in a vast market newly sprung amongst the dwarf birches. Deals were made and marriages arranged as blood alliances between the families. There were even entertainers to juggle and tumble, and music came from horn and string. Here and there a crowd surrounded a teller of tales, his voice lilting through the sung-poems of ritualised history and myth, each weaving intricate patterns through the other to blend into a memorable whole. All proceedings of a city were now occurring on the plain by the lake, for Iceland had no city. Here, for a little while, the nation in the pangs of birth had a capital city of tents, of temporary shelters and booths. And it was here by common consent for no lord had issued the summons.

The goði saw a known face in the crowd. He shouted his name, and added, 'Prosperity to your hall.'

'And upon yours, Goði. How was your journey?'

'Long and good. Is this your son? He has grown to a man! I have two fine young daughters.'

'Are your sheep stronger since I sold you the good ram?'

'Yes, they are better for the winter. Has Ulfljót arrived?'

'It is said that he will come tomorrow. Tomorrow he will bring the law.'

'Tomorrow we shall have our own law,' said the goði, not to inform but to confirm the miracle, for all knew the purpose of this meeting. The land had been seized and now the people were to be governed, not by the whim of men but by the power of law; law to keep free men free from the oppression of the strong for it had the strength of the majority welded into its heart. Ulfljót the Scholar had been sent to Norway by the will of the people to learn the ways of law and to adapt it to the ways of Iceland; and now he was home and would tell them of his findings. Tomorrow he would lay the law before the people for their perusal. Tomorrow would be a great day, the greatest day that anyone present would ever know.

The morning of the first Althing was still as the elected of the people, the thirty-six goðar, each with his two advisers, composed themselves before a flat-topped rock to await the com-

ing of Ulfljót the Lawspeaker. Horses and cattle had been
sacrificed that the gods might smile upon this assembly and
make fruitful its deliberations.

Voices were stilled as the Lawspeaker appeared and quietly
mounted the rock. The reverence was not for the man, who
was merely the vessel, but for the law contained within the
man. He it was who knew the law and would recite it from
memory for the ears of the people. As the singers of sagas
were their records of history, so the Lawspeaker was the
record and signpost for their present and future dealings
with men and gods. Power resided in the goðar, but the Lawspeaker restrained them and directed the way of the individual by uniting him with the whole.

Ulfljót raised his arms towards the assembled people, drawing them together in unity. He spoke, and the sound of his
voice reverberated from the rock wall behind. It sang over the
plain of Thingvellir, out over the ice, and in the hearts of free
men throughout all time.

'This is the Law of the People . . .'

In a world of kings and despots the first republic of the north
had been born, and the first parliament the world had known
was now in session.

Dwarf birch is not the easiest wood in the world to light so I
settled for a breakfast of biscuits washed down with clear
lake-water. The track led on for a couple of miles with the lake
to my left and the plain of Thingvellir stretching to my right. It
was yet quite cool and circular ripples on the water's still
surface denoted the presence of breakfasting fish. Before me,
in the distance, arose a long wall of rock where the earth in a
long-past time had shrugged a little. A waterfall dropped
clearly from its top to the green plain thirty feet below, a still
white streak punctuating the length of grey-black rock like an
exclamation mark. An hour of strolling later I stood in the

influence of the wall of riven lava and walked the well-trod path along its length. There was a large rock, perhaps ten feet high, smoothed by the rubbing of boots. Its top was flat and easy of access so I sat there for a while to rest, alone in the morning. The view was fine over the vast emptiness of the plain with the geyser still spurting beyond the lake and being reflected in its waters; as pleasing a sight as I have ever seen, the sort to bring tranquillity to the minds of men. I nodded to myself as thoughts of history wafted through my head, nodded again and, rejoining the path, walked on towards the cleft in the hills that led to Reykjavik.

It was midday when I passed through the gap and found myself on a well frequented road through rolling moorland, the equivalent of the moor that had confronted me at the beginning of the trek so many ages before. Maybe on a clear day it would have been possible to see the sea, but the morning's clarity had been swamped by a cold, clammy ground-mist through which rain began to fall, driven by a half-hearted and weary breeze, as if the gods of Iceland had ceded defeat but had not yet left the field. It was not strolling weather and I quickened my pace. It had been my intention to camp before Reykjavik leaving a gentle walk for the morning, but the capital was a mere fifteen miles distant and the prospect of a hot meal that evening spurred me into a marching step. Despite the falling water and swirling mist happy marching songs bounced on my brain as, like a circus performer atop a great ball, my feet pushed the sphere back upon its axis so that I could stand at the requisite point thereon. Once I got the ball moving it became easier and the miles sped back.

In mid-afternoon the track became a metalled road and soon after this the mist lifted revealing, less than ten miles distant, the gleaming buildings of Reykjavik with the bay of mists before it and the Denmark Strait beyond. Here was the western shore! I had done it! I was very, very happy.

Traffic was heavy on the motorway that the road quickly

became so I walked along the footpath-cum-cycle-track beside the roaring stream of canned humanity. I wanted to shout to them of my triumph, but they were utterly oblivious with their minds on more immediate matters. Within the city I found a camp-site and set up my mini-camp amid the masses of large orange tents. Then I washed myself thoroughly in *hot* water and changed to my cleanest dirty clothes. Tonight was to be a night of celebration. First a massive meal, then I was going to the pictures.

Hair clean, still coldly damp, and more or less neatly combed, I consumed consommé with croutons and a beer, followed it with lamb in an utterly ambrosaic cheese sauce surrounded by succulent vegetation, and a beer, after which I demolished a large piece of gâteau with fresh cream, and a beer, and finished with cheese and biscuits, which I washed down with a beer. I paid, trying very hard not to look at the first digit on the bill.

The cinema I wished to visit was a small family affair at Hellusundi 6a run by one Villi Knudsen who, like his father Osvaldur before him, made a career out of filming all volcanic activity in Iceland and showing it in his cinema for the delight of tourists. His advertising had told me that the cinema was closed on Sundays and Mondays, so, it being Saturday and my flight leaving on Tuesday, it was tonight or never.

The auditorium was small and there was a church-hall air about the rapidly filling room. I had seen very little film of volcanic activity, such events not being considered entertaining by Hollywood, the BBC or the ITA. The excellent programme consisted of several short films concerning the many recent eruptions. The island of Surtsey rose spectacularly from the sea before my widening eyes, and the island of Heimaey was reshaped and its town half destroyed on film taken in 1973 as nature rode unheeding over the careful works of man. But it was the eruption of Hekla in 1981 that captured my mind. I saw the wall of aa lava, the stone forest beneath which I had slept prior to my ascent of the volcano. On the film it was glowing red and smoking blackly as it crawled inexorably over the land at a mile every hour, great smouldering boulders falling from its ten-foot-high crest to crash amongst the blanket of tephra at its foot. As I watched the molten lava belched great gobbets of liquid rock upwards, where they solidified and remained as the petrified forests of Hekla to scar those who would dare to climb her slopes. Running rivers of fire ran from her vents, and at night they shone like neon. Such might is difficult to come to terms with in a small cinema amid gasping tourists.

I spoke to Villi after the show and we discussed his and my filming. He was a capable gentleman interested in life in all its aspects.

'Would you not like to film volcanic eruptions?' he wished to know. Nothing, I intimated, would give me greater pleasure; but it had been some time since one had occurred in Salford.

'There is a fissure, near the Midge-lake, Mývatn, that I have been expecting to erupt for ten years. I have had three film crews standing by all this time. Some day it must blow. When it does, give me a ring and we will film it together.' He said it with a smile, but I knew that he meant it. I explained that, sadly, I would be in England in three days. The chances of it blowing in the meantime, we agreed, were remote indeed.

'Phone me!' he insisted. 'Phone me if it goes!'

We shook hands and parted, smiling. On rapidly stiffening legs I walked back to the camp-site through a Saturday night city which at ten-thirty was already deserted. 'What *do* they get up to,' I wondered, 'when they close their front doors?'

It was a very Christian Sunday, empty and joyless. First I had to make official my crossing by dipping my feet into the western sea upon this, the twenty-fourth day; so with camera in hand containing a whole minute of film with which to record the event, I walked the ghostly morning streets of Reykjavik. Not even a dog did I encounter for it is illegal to own a canine companion in Reykjavik. Indeed they may, quite legitimately, be shot on sight by the police. The pavements and parks, the children, the shoes and the carpets of Iceland's capital are doggie-dung free.

Cleanliness was also evident in the pollution-free air for the Icelanders need no power-stations fuelled by coal to heat their homes. About fifty years ago they began to harness the naturally hot spring-water and after much experimentation in the capital they found the best system. Two great pipelines, each ten miles long and heavily insulated, run from springs outside the city, carrying the almost boiling water to storage tanks in the city, from where it is distributed to individual homes, hotels, schools and other buildings to heat them and to pour from their taps. So well insulated is the system that only about ten per cent of the original heat is lost in transit. This is yet another example of the Icelanders' resourcefulness and has given rise to the growing, in spring-heated greenhouses, of fruit, vegetables and even flowers, which it would be impossible to grow outdoors. Indeed the new town of Hveragerði thirty miles south-east of Reykjavik was built around this aspect of the Icelandic economy.

Reykjavik has expanded rapidly since the turn of the century when it was a mere fishing village of some six thousand souls. Now it houses 118,000 people and a well-planned building programme is spreading the city out to the hinterland. Buildings tend to be low and earthquake-proof.

Policemen were not in evidence. I realised that I did not know what an Icelandic policeman looked like for I had never seen one. Right on cue a police-car, black and white, and festooned with lights and signs, flashed by on enormous balloon tyres. It passed so quickly that I did not see its occupants so to this day I have no idea of the appearance of an

Icelandic copper, a fact which speaks highly of the social conscience of the citizenry.

Feet were dipped, and the fact recorded on film. I made a prearranged phone-call (reversed charges) to Radio Manchester to inform the people of my own city of my safe arrival. I had thought little of home for the month past, as is my wont when engaged in an expedition, for the intensity of expedition life is such that to diversify one's thoughts and emotions is to enhance whatever dangers may lurk unseen. Now was the time to remove the armour and allow normality to seep back into the soul. I thought of home, and people, and my roots in the land. Of the beauties of Iceland, too, I thought; of glacier and waterfall, of northern lights and the view from Hekla, none of which were to be seen in England. But did Iceland have dark forests and the crisp red leaves of autumn, and where in this young land were the bones of truly remote ancestors? Yes, I recognised the feeling. The traveller, the avowed internationalist, the wanderer o'er the face of the earth, was homesick.

All that Sunday, and the following day, I wandered the wide streets of Reykjavik. There were presents to buy, and souvenirs, and post-cards to send. Suddenly I was on holiday; I was a tourist picking the trinkets from the tray of goodies. But it was an uneasy holiday. I wanted Tuesday and England. Like a bird on a wire I was poised for flight.

Since the airport bus left the Reykjavik terminal at six a.m. I spent the night of Monday on the same patch of grass I occupied for my first night in Iceland. The rain, dutifully, fell as I thought of the trip. Other than the accomplishment of what I believed to be the first coast-to-coast walk, the joys of vistas and the cash for the children's hospital, had I achieved anything worthwhile? I concluded that for mankind in general I had achieved nothing of consequence other than a further confirmation that a man alone, if he knows the ropes, can achieve things said to be impossible. It is a strange quirk of the mind that I always find a trip to be impossible in retrospect, never in prospect. There was film of the journey for the edification of future generations, and a tape diary to prompt the coming months of writing. But mostly there had been confirmed within me, somewhere deep and difficult of access, the underlying connections between the peoples who roam our planet, who find places to stay awhile, and then move on; for it is always in part that they move, leaving behind their blood in those who remain to mingle with the ones who come after. We are indeed a single family, no matter how distant the cousins. Perhaps I would return to this struggling young land still fighting to retain its freedom, now with an economic sword. Then again, perhaps I would not. There are many cousins to visit for I belong to a vast and diverse family.

Ah, but the time had come to return to the hearth of my own branch. Joyfully I packed my rucksack in the rain and walked to the airport bus. There were thoughts of familiar tastes, of steak pudding and chips with mushy peas all salted and swimming in vinegar, of eggs-bacon-and-beans with buttered toast, of darkly golden tea swirling in a mug, of traditional Lancashire beef biryani with pillau rice and pappadums dripping with mango chutney, of foaming real-ale tangy with hops and smooth to the throat.

Of the latter I thought a great deal.

Postscript

Mail awaited my return; mountains of mail, much of which had been caught up in a postal strike prior to my departure and consequently should have been read before the trip. There was information and encouragement, and the usual discouraging but well-meant advice that the trip was impossible and should not be attempted alone. Such words, though meant to discourage, always strengthen my resolve since the danger does not merely add spice to the trip, it is one of the most important elements. The whole thing is like a game of skill between Old Baldie and me, with life placed in pawn for the prize. Such a prize is of limited value as it is already the property of my adversary and merely mine on loan, so the reason for the game must be the game itself with its joyful victories and sad defeats, and without the challenge of danger there would be no game at all. To hit a ball with foot, hand or stick, no matter how skilfully, is a game for children, for what is the challenge, what the stake, and what the goal?

As to my belief that mine was the first coast-to-coast walk across Iceland, general expert opinion seemed to be that it would be difficult to prove, but in all probability it was. More than this, however, I had proved that such a journey was possible; and that was my victory for what I had pioneered others could accomplish also, with perhaps more scientific goals.

Now Orlog, what the Vikings called the impersonal power of fate, is surely the grandfather of perversity. Within a day or so after my return there appeared upon a TV screen news of a mighty volcanic eruption in Iceland, near, the announcer said, to a lake called Mývatn. The lava flowed magnificently before my eyes as I heaped curses upon Orlog, and the minions of Orlog. I could picture the gleeful face of Villi Knudsen, who undoubtedly took the film, as his ten-year wait for the eruption ended. 'Phone me!' I could hear him say. 'Phone me if it goes!' I had missed the chance of a lifetime by a matter of hours.

But time moveth on. There were other games to play, and the playing field was mighty. Deserts there were, and wild savannas; cold steppes and steaming jungles. The grass beyond the hill is rarely greener than in my green and pleasant land ... but *by gum* it's a lot more interesting.

Interest, speculation, finance and desire danced together a cerebral quadrille as ideas distilled from chaos. When I was ready I took an empty file and wrote upon the spine in thick black letters. Then I smiled.

And doubtless, too, did Old Baldie.